Music in Education

MUSIC IN EDUCATION
A point of view

Arnold Bentley

NFER Publishing Company Ltd.

Published by the NFER Publishing Company Ltd.,
Book Division, 2 Jennings Buildings, Thames Avenue,
Windsor, Berks. SL4 1QS
Registered Office: The Mere, Upton Park, Slough, Berks. SL1 2DQ
First published 1975
© Arnold Bentley, 1975
ISBN 85633 066 3

Printed in Great Britain by
John Gardner (Printers) Ltd., Hawthorne Road, Bootle, Merseyside L20 6JX
Distributed in the USA by Humanities Press Inc.,
Hillary House-Fernhill House, Atlantic Highlands,
New Jersey 07716 USA

Contents

PREFACE

The sub-title—a point of view—calls for explanation. This book is about music education that takes place, or might take place, mainly in schools and associated institutions. Even within that limitation, and even if it were written by several people, it could not be comprehensive; written by one person it is inevitably even less so. As with religion, politics and general education, everyone may hold a personal point of view about music and thus about music education. At the present time, through radio, television, disc and taped records, music is almost everywhere, often when and where many people would prefer to be without it: on railway stations, in aircraft, even in coaches. At the level of hearing, if not attentive listening, and as distinct from personal participation, it is more pervasive than most other phenomena of existence. Thus everyone, or almost everyone, has some sort of attitude towards it. It would therefore be arrogant of me to presume to express more than a personal point of view, and this is all I offer.

This point of view has been reached through many years experience of teaching children of all ages in schools, of trying to help students preparing themselves to be teachers in Training Colleges (now Colleges of Education) and postgraduates in University, through contacts with other teachers not only in this country but in and from most other countries of the world, and through my own research and that of others.

Such experience has, I hope, broadened my own horizon, and it has also, inevitably, helped me to distil or crystallize my point of view. Equally inevitably, and because I am as humanly fallible as anyone else, my point of view is a personal one, with which some may agree; many may not. When people disagree with points of view on human affairs they are inclined to label them as biased, even as prejudiced. That is a risk that must be taken. I claim neither omniscience nor final authority.

Because I am largely expressing a personal point of view I have avoided the not uncommon practice of using third person technique: 'the writer opines, considers, etc.' Instead, in order to try to communicate more directly and personally with the reader, I simply say 'I think', 'I believe' etc.; this is not arrogance—I do not use the expression 'I *know*'.

Chapter One

Music: its place in education

Consider man and music. Music may exist apart from man as in the idea of the music of the spheres, but ordinary man cannot hear this. Music for music's sake, like art for art's sake, will have no consideration in the following pages. Rather shall we be concerned with music for man's sake, accepting that it is only in terms of what he hears that music can have any meaning for man.

Education is entirely concerned with man; it may have been noticed that the order of the opening sentence of the above paragraph was man first, followed by music. Since we shall be concerned with education in the earlier years, for man read children.

Our thoughts will also be directed mainly to education in schools, but not ignoring home environment and musical education that takes place outside school.

In the history of mankind, schooling is a comparatively recent phenomenon, and in our own country compulsory attendance at school for all children is barely one hundred years old.

The word 'compulsory' implies great responsibilities for those who provide the education, or schooling, because they must decide the content of it. The younger children in school have little choice; firstly they must attend. Also, in spite of current ideas of freedom in the schoolroom, fundamentally they have only limited choice of activities. For example, it is the adult educators who establish such objectives as learning to speak intelligibly, to read and write, and to use numbers. These tools of communication are regarded as essentials of living in the society of one's fellows.

Other objectives, and activities intended to achieve them, have been introduced, and it is interesting to note that one of the earliest of these, since education in school became compulsory for all children, was music. Admittedly, music in the schoolroom of a hundred years ago was different from much of what happens today. There were few, if any, instruments and the scope was restricted to the music the children and their teachers could make themselves with their voices. One of the reasons given for introducing music was to bring a little light and joy into what apparently was considered to be the rather serious, and dreary, existence of 19th century Board School children. The success of this cannot be measured, but we should note that any light and joy was to be achieved through the children making music themselves. The gramophone, tape recorder and TV did not exist.

It was made the responsibility of the educators, the teachers in the schoolroom, to provide education, not only in the three 'r's, but also in music, within the limitions that existed. Singing was the obvious means of doing this, in most cases the only means. But the limitations may have had their compensations: We tend to sing when we are happy; and taking part in singing can, in not too inappropriate circumstances, help us to feel happier than we were. Witness the last night of the Promenade Concerts, *Songs of Praise* on BBC television, crowd singing at football matches and other big assemblies. On these occasions even those who might rarely sing or hum alone, even in the bathroom whose resonance encourages vocalization, are found to be joining in, and presumably feeling no worse for it.

Whether all children enjoyed singing in the 19th century schoolroom we cannot know. But apparently many did, if we are to judge by the flourishing adult choral societies of that period. Their attitudes to music, positive or otherwise, were being formed.

Attitudes

Success or otherwise in music education, or in any other activity in school, depends largely upon the attitudes of pupils and teachers. A positive attitude has a chance of resulting in some degree of success; a negative attitude must result in failure. Attitudes of individuals are conditioned largely by environment, opportunity and the quality of motivation supplied by the teacher, possibly even by genetic endowment. We cannot measure, separately, environmental and genetic influences, the one 'uncontaminated' by the other. We can control the environment, to some extent; but we can never be sure that we are aware of all the aspects of it, and we are even less sure that we are isolating any one of those aspects, in order to assess its influence, and at the same time holding all other aspects constant. Compound this uncertainty with the admission of the possibility of genetic influence, which we do not know how to measure with any degree of confidence, and we end up with a fair amount of guesswork which we hope is inspired or at least intelligent.

We can never be absolutely sure what are the causes of attitudes. For example, how can we explain with certainty the different attitudes towards, and abilities in, music on the part of children in the same family, all given similar wide opportunities, facilities and parental encouragement? One child, not necessarily the eldest, becomes interested, wants to play the violin at an early age and makes rapid progress. Another tries, but makes only slow progress, and in spite of encouragement gives it up. Another shows no evidence of interest at all in music. Even home environment is not all-persuasive. It looks as though some other influence may be operating, call it personality, genetic endowment or what we will.

A comparable, but more diffuse, picture may be seen in the schoolroom, with not three or four but thirty-three or thirty-four children, reacting sometimes together with the teacher, reacting always upon each other. Each one is further influenced by his own personality and home environment. In this even less individually persuasive situation than the home environment the teacher sets out to create positive attitudes to learning in many areas. It is the teacher who sets the goals and by diverse means encourages the children to try to achieve them. They will move along the road towards those goals at different speeds, with some scarcely moving at all, and others moving fast. We can guess at the reasons for relative successes and failures, but we can rarely be sure, however hard we try to *know*. Furthermore, the attitude of a child to any area of learning (or subject, to use a somewhat old-fashioned word) will depend to some extent on the degree of success he achieves in that area.

Whilst it is difficult to *know*, i.e. be sure about, the reasons for success/ failure, or varying rates of progress, the reason for music preference differences between the sexes, at quite early ages, is also elusive. Some interesting evidence about the different attitudes of boys and girls towards music was obtained from a survey in 1971/72.* Eight hundred children aged 9 to 11 years, in 20 primary schools in a city area in NW England and an urban-plus-rural area in the South, responded to a questionnaire on attitudes. The children did not disclose their names, so

* Information obtained from a survey which was made during a Reading University/Schools Council project on Music Education of Young Children, not published at time of writing.

any implication that they should give responses that would meet with their own teachers' approval was removed. The number, 800, was not particularly large, but it may be regarded as a fair sample of boys and girls in different parts of the country and from wide socioeconomic/cultural backgrounds.

There are dangers in generalizing from any sample, and nothing was *proved;* but the evidence obtained does reveal certain attitudinal tendencies, especially as between the boys and girls. It looks as though the girls were *generally* more favourably disposed to music than the boys. More girls than boys had regular instrumental lessons, more girls sang in school choirs. Both sexes ranked singing and playing instruments higher than any other aspect of music, but the girls ranked singing marginally higher than instrumental playing, whilst the boys preferred the reverse. Music and movement was high on the girls' list of preferences, firmly at the bottom for boys. The boys recorded high preferences for the sounds of trumpet and drum; the girls put the sounds of these two at the bottom of their list of preferences but gave high choice to the sounds of piano and clarinet. The sound of the recorder was lowest, out of seven instrumental sounds, for boys, and fourth for girls. When asked if they liked singing hymns, 62 per cent of the boys and 79 per cent of the girls replied in the affirmative.

These are only a few of the pieces of information obtained from the survey. They *prove* nothing, least of all that *all* girls are more favourably disposed to music than *all* boys; or, for instance, that girls like singing and boys do not. Nothing could be further from the truth: Otherwise there would be no male choristers of any age. However, they do provide numerical, proportional indication of the attitudes of the children sampled, attitudes not overlooked by many an observant teacher.

Such attitudes must depend to a large extent upon the experience that school and home have already provided. Yet in school, where these boys and girls had been, and were still being, taught together, why the sex preference differences at this early age? We do not know.

General education

Let us briefly consider education in general, and then music education in particular.

The first few months of a child's life appear to be limited almost entirely to the basic needs of existence, mainly associated with the mother, and the beginning of noticing and reacting to his environment.

His horizon rapidly expands with increasing age, and it is possible that he experiences and learns more new things in his first five years than in all the rest of his life.

This expansion of experience and learning seems to continue to be rapid until about the ninth or tenth year, during, say, the first four or five years in school. From about then on, even to the end of his life, he continues to have new experiences, but he appears to become more selective, gradually at first but increasingly so with time. He is learning what are his personal strengths and weaknesses, not only through self-assessment but also by comparing himself with his fellows.* What he finds he can not do successfully he tends to avoid. Towards situations with which he can cope his attitude is likely to be positive; towards those situations in which he encounters relative failure it is likely to be negative.

This process continues into, and throughout, adult life. How else could we account for the enormous variety of wage/salary earning occupations in spite of environmental limitations and the multifarious ways in which spare time is used?

The pattern of education, in terms of schooling and associated activities, seems to accept, complement and mirror this developmental/ maturational process. It also influences to a greater or less extent the developmental aspect.

As a result in the nursery school (up to 5 years of age) and in the infant school (5 to 7/8 years), the child is provided with a wide range of experiences in many areas of learning: 'learning situations' are devised in order that he may extend his range of experiences. The method may be mainly through play, but we should not forget that the young child often treats his play very seriously. Every new experience in life, whether in school or outside, is a challenge which he meets with varying degrees of success. 'Degrees of success' also implies degrees of failure. In terms of human activities and experiences, this must be accepted. We try to avoid putting a child in situations where he is likely to fail, but neither we, nor he, can know whether he will succeed, or fail, until we have given him an opportunity to try himself out. Thus, as wide a range as possible of familiar and new experiences is given in the nursery and infant schools.

* ' "How am I doing?" is often asked. The individual does not only assess himself but throws out clues to others and learns about himself from the responses.' (Shipman, M. D., 1972, p.30.)

A similar wide range of experiences is given in the next stage of schooling: the junior school (ages 7/8 to 11), or, in some districts, the middle school (up to 12/13). However, during this stage, we begin to observe more pronounced individual reactions to the experiences provided, for instance in reading, writing, number, in art, in games and other physical activities, and in music. Ideally, we give extra help to those experiencing difficulties, and we provide additional challenges to the more able. But, whatever the cause, nature or nurture, the differences in reactions to, and abilities in, various activities are patently obvious. Nothing is gained by pretending that these differences do not exist.

We adults, and equally children, in school and outside it, tend to like that which we can do successfully, and increasingly to dislike and to avoid that in which we have little or no success, in other words fail. Hence the reason for trying to devise experiences in which the child is likely to succeed, with the hope, perhaps even the expectation, that he will increasingly like that experience. However it is important that we should be honest, and admit that none of us has yet succeeded in devising a range of experiences in which every child achieves equal success.

Thus, in the junior or middle school stage we increasingly observe varying degrees of success/failure, which are reflected in the adoption by pupils of varying attitudes to different experiences, or subjects. These variations of attitudes appear to become more marked with increasing age, and to continue even more markedly in the secondary school (11 or 13 to 18/19 yrs).

We might liken the process of education in school and associated activities to a triangle of experiences, broad-based and then narrowing towards the apex, but never closing to one single peak. (Even in advancing years we still seek, or are involuntarily challenged by, some new experiences.)

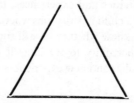

Or we might liken the process of education to a sieve which retains the big pieces (our strengths) and gradually allows the smaller pieces (our weaknesses) to fall through.

Music education

What happens in life, and in education in general, also applies in music education.

We, who find that music makes a great contribution to our lives, not unnaturally would like as many people as possible to share the emotional/intellectual satisfaction it gives us. We do all in our power to make that possible. At the same time we have to be realistic, and face the quite obvious fact that music, especially as we may think of and react to it, is not for many, or even most, of our adult contemporaries. Their attitudes towards music have also been forming throughout life. (We know that attitudes sometimes change, but there is no easily discernible systematic pattern in such changes.)

Sometimes older pupils in their early teens, even those who like and are good at music, drop it as a subject in school. This reflects attitudes towards priorities; other subjects have become more important to them at that stage of development, time is limited, and choices are made. This is a fact of living. Respect for the individual young person's attitude and choice is important; he may need advice, guidance and even persuasion, but ultimately the choice of life style—professional/occupational/recreational—will be his.

I have spoken of attitudes arising from the discovery of strengths and weaknesses, success or failure. These are discovered through experience, which involves challenge and testing. Currently there are those who apparently disapprove of such words as testing and failure; even of success. None shall be better than the rest; competition, tests, examinations are out. Yet even these people allow exceptions, for instance in physical activities: athletics and games. Without any prompting by adults, children will test themselves to see who can run faster, climb higher, throw a ball farther, score more goals. Through their own play they virtually select themselves for first-eleven soccer or cricket teams. (And woe betide the games master or mistress who selects individuals for such teams that the pupils consider are not as good at the game as others not selected!) Competition, entirely unprompted by adults, appears to be an integral feature in many aspects of children's spontaneous play. Furthermore, they soon learn to accept that some are better at whatever they are doing than others.

Such acceptance is an important feature of life. One gradually learns what one can do, and what one cannot do. If I, now past middle age, tried to run a four-minute mile, I should not only fail to complete the distance in the time, but, having started and tried to maintain the requisite speed, I should probably be dead before I reached half way. Acceptance of this fact—however unpalatable it might be, which it is not—is a condition of my hoped-for continued survival! This example may be considered somewhat extreme, but, in less spectacular ways, life, one's very existence, depends upon such acceptances. And so, certainly, does happiness and contentment. The acceptance that some are more successful at certain activities, physical or mental, than one's self, and some less successful, is a by no means unimportant aspect of growing up and continued living. Children learn it in association with their fellows, even without formal class order lists or formal testing and examinations.

However, these latter do have their uses. They indicate what an individual can do, in terms of what he is asked to do, at a given moment of time. They indicate ability: again, what the individual can do. This may depend upon something innate, upon industriousness and its opposite, laziness, or upon many other factors; but that again is life. Industriousness or laziness will depend to some extent upon the motivation (i.e. the interest aroused *and* maintained) by the teacher, but it probably depends also upon many other factors that cannot be measured quantitatively, or even speculated upon, with any degree of accuracy.

Even the most anti-examination, anti-test, anti-success/failure egalitarian enthusiasts appear to accept that music, particularly instrumental playing, solo singing and/or composition, is a special case. Given early and reasonable experiences and facilities, children soon discover for themselves who is 'better' in musical skills than the majority; and most people would agree that the earlier any performing ability, aptitude, or talent is discovered, the better for the child. The important phrase in the foregoing sentence is 'given early and reasonable experiences and facilities'. Without these, aptitude is unlikely to be discovered, and potential strengths ignored.* When a child has no opportunity of discovering his strengths in music his attitude towards music is likely to be negative or at best indifferent.

Thus, ideally, the pattern of music education in school, as I see it, would seem to be as follows. Throughout the nursery and primary school/middle school (3/4 to 12/13 years) we provide the widest possible experiences of music, from the base of our triangle upwards, but expecting, and accepting, that individual preferences and attitudes, however they arise, will gradually reduce the variety of activities of the

* More will be said about this in Chapter 5 on 'Measuring Musical Abilities'.

individual child as he grows older. One child will reveal weaknesses in some aspects of music education, and of course we try to help him to overcome these; another will reveal exceptional strengths and enthusiasms, and to develop these he should be given all possible assistance; and there will be a whole continuum of varying abilities and attitudes between these extremes. Dealing with this range is one of the main problems of teaching music in classes or groups of children.

Motivation and the personality of the teacher

I have spoken of early and reasonable experiences and facilities, and of the motivation, i.e. the interest aroused and maintained by the teacher. The provision of experiences and facilities by the teacher implies that the teacher must possess adequate knowledge and skills. These need not be academically extensive for dealing with young children. Obviously the greater the knowledge and skills the better. But the fact must be faced that relatively few nursery and primary school teachers possess great knowledge about, and even less expertise in, music. This is not a criticism of this body of teachers; they have much else with which to concern themselves besides music. However the more they can apply, imaginatively, such knowledge and skills as they possess, the more extensive will be the range of experience they can provide.

Whilst motivation, i.e. the interest aroused and maintained, obviously depends upon the teacher's knowledge and skills, it also depends upon an additional factor often referred to as the personality of the teacher. Many highly qualified musicians are not particularly successful teachers, especially in the classroom. Neither is there any moral or other reason why they should be, if they are not that kind of person. At any conference of educationists, music or otherwise, methods and content may form the major areas of discussion, but, whatever agreement or disagreement there may be about these, almost inevitably it is ultimately agreed that all depends upon the personality of the teacher.

What does this expression, the personality of the teacher, mean? One may list various desirable attributes, but a clear and simple definition of the personality (in the singular) is elusive. Successful teachers may vary enormously in their personalities; they may not all even love children (an attribute that is sometimes given high priority). But to be a successful teacher of children it would appear that, whatever the extent of their knowledge and skills, whatever their other diverse personality traits, they must be at least as interested in the pupils they teach as in the subject(s) they profess. Given such interest in their pupils, they are likely to make the mind-to-mind contact which is basic to any education; without it, they are not.

Suitable personality for teaching is the most difficult aspect to assess in selecting musicians for training as teachers of music in school. The assessment of musical knowledge and skills is infinitely easier and more objective. There is no fool-proof criterion for assessing suitable personality. Seeking answers to such questions as 'would I be happy to have this person teaching my own offspring?' or 'could I recommend this person to a headmaster friend?' may help. Psychologically devised personality tests can provide more objective answers. But ultimately one resorts to a subjective, horse-sense decision. It may not be entirely satisfactory, but on the whole it works.

Experience of graduate musicians in training as teachers clearly reveals one thing: That the person who is entirely wrapped up in himself and music, however good as a musician, rarely becomes a successful teacher in school. 'Me and my music' is not the best attitude for the teacher. Rather must it be: 'The children I teach and what I, as a musician, can contribute to their education'. Such an attitude is at least propitious for the arousal and maintenance of interest in music; furthermore it does not necessitate neglect of one's own personal musicianship.

Again, we find ourselves referring to attitudes; in this case the general attitude of the teacher which in turn must affect, positively, negatively, or somewhere between these poles, the attitudes of the pupils.

Intellect and emotions: education and entertainment

Music is usually regarded as something to be enjoyed by the listener, or by the more active participant, who of course is also a listener. It is mainly an aural experience that is usually, though not always, in some degree pleasurable. It is enjoyed by different people in many different ways, and by some, apparently and upon their own evidence, not at all.

The aim of music education is sometimes expressed as: 'to make children love music', or 'to make children enjoy music'. This is nonsense. We cannot make children, or adults, love or enjoy anything. All we can do is to provide opportunities. Love, enjoyment, pleasure, are not realistic objectives. Of course we hope that these may, even will, occur, but we cannot teach them. We can devise learning situations, create opportunities, teach in a way in which love, enjoyment and pleasure may happen; but we can not ensure such end results.

Some children apparently enjoy and love chemistry, or mathematics (or many other school activities that some other children do not enjoy and certainly do not love). Why is this? Doubtless successful teachers are enthusiasts for their subjects, but do they express their aims as to make children love mathematics or chemistry, or set out to give them a good time in their lessons? I suggest that their aim is rather that the children should learn some mathematics or chemistry; and they teach with that end in view. Incidentally, 'learning situations', an expression currently much used, are by no means a new idea; practical work in mathematics and experimental work in the science laboratory (the latter carefully designed devised and controlled for the sake of physical safety!) carried out by the pupils themselves, were taking place in schools long before the expression 'learning situations' was coined. The teachers taught, and still must teach, the subject, discipline, area of learning, or whatever we call it. Obviously they must arouse and maintain interest, an essential prerequisite of anything that is to be taught and learnt. I propose interest as a more fundamental aim than love, enjoyment, pleasure; there will not be much of these without interest. What is more, interest is not aroused and maintained merely by trying to make things soft, easy, unchallenging and undemanding, but rather, bearing in mind the age and stage of development of the pupils, by getting stuck into the basic stuff of the subject.

If we can arouse a child's interest in music, and thereafter help him to acquire some skill in it, so that he may continue to develop that interest, there is a good chance that he may come to enjoy it, even to love it; but we can never be sure of this.

Love and enjoyment are commonly associated with emotion, with the implication that emotion and intellect are opposites. Such polarization can be misleading. Emotion and intellect are not wholly discrete opposites. When we think about something (the intellectual aspect) it is difficult not to become emotionally involved, positively or negatively. This even applies to research, however objective we try to be. It also applies to music, as it does to many other phenomena of life. Even if the initial impact is primarily emotional, which may involve immediate like or dislike, as is often suggested to be the case with music, we still tend to think about it. Admittedly, if intense dislike is the only reaction we may dismiss the experience and think no more about it. However if we find the experience of some interest, even if initially we do not actively like it, we tend to think about it. The more we think about it, and the more we become actively involved, the more are we likely to make it a part of us, begin to understand it, perhaps to appreciate it, maybe enjoy it, even love it; or the opposite!

Education is to make a difference. If that is not accepted, what is the point of an elaborate and expensive educational system, and of compelling all children to spend some eleven years of their lives in schools? In the making of the difference the educators have great responsibility; furthermore, a worthwhile difference will not be made without some effort on the part of both teachers and pupils. A major part of such effort is in the intellectual (thinking) sphere. Education that has no intellectual content, *at the level appropriate to the age and stage of development of the child,* is no education. This applies to music education, as to other areas of learning. Mere entertainment, sometimes pretty mindless entertainment as seen in some class music lessons in school, can scarcely justify the use of the term education. It appears to arise from an idea that music must be an effortless relaxation from other more demanding subjects. Judged by the obvious boredom of many pupils, the idea is baseless.

Value of music education?

Most people would subscribe to the value of learning to read words, and to handle number; these are means of communication and of coping with certain essentials of living. They are useful. Except for a tiny minority of any society, music has no such utility value in terms of wage or salary earning. Neither do we use it in order to communicate our needs for the essentials of maintaining life. We could contrive to exist without it; doubtless there are those who do so.

Various philosophers at different times have expressed differing views about its place in the scheme of living. These views can be read elsewhere and I do not propose to argue about them; nor about 'music for its own sake', which might be expressed more realistically as 'music for man's sake'. For without man, where would be the music?

However, claims have been made for a place for music in education by practising educators who would not regard themselves as philosophers, and who are not all primarily or professionally musicians. Let us consider a few of these claims, and the kind of music education referred to.

In the last few years experiments have been made, particularly in Hungary, by musicians, psychologists, medical experts and other educators, which suggest that music education on the Kodaly principles (which fundamentally are similar to those of John Curwen in the 19th century) stimulates the cortex and results in improved performance in non-musical intellectual and physical activities, and in beneficial social development (Sandor, F. (ed.), 1966, 1969; Ribière-Raverlat, J., 1971). With such factors as age and social background under careful control, the results indicated that children in the music primary schools having six music lessons a week (and thus fewer lessons in other subjects) eventually scored better in non-musical subjects and activities than children from other schools in which only two lessons a week were given in music and more time was devoted to the other subjects. As in all research into human activities there is no absolute proof; and the experimental methods have been challenged. However, such is the evidence produced that it looks as though there may be something in the idea that the kind of music education referred to results in enhanced learning in other spheres.

Another example of the advantage claimed for music education is contained in the Preface of our own Choir Schools Directory:

> The academic results of pupils at Choir Schools are good .... The intellectual discipline and training of the Choir sharpens the wits and is a firm foundation for academic success. No other activity in which a boy regularly takes part requires such concentration, attention to detail, and, above all, sense of awareness, as the daily performance of complex music which must be judged entirely by adult standards.

This statement does not claim that all boy choristers in choir schools produce better academic results than non-choristers in choir schools, or than boys in other preparatory schools. Statistics on comparable academic performance are not available; but observation indicates that, in general, little boy choristers who spend perhaps two hours daily in singing (practices and services) do as well as, and often better, in non-musical academic activities, than boys who have more time for other activities but do not have this musical education, which may indeed 'sharpen the wits', although we cannot prove it.

Going back further, we find Brownlow (1858) writing about music at the Foundling Hospital in 1847:

> As a considerable portion of the time allotted to the practice of music is drawn from the ordinary school hours, great care has, also,

been taken to ascertain how far the band-boys are—when brought in competition at the annual school examination with other boys not in the band—affected by this arrangement, and the results have shown that a full proportion of the prizes, awarded for scholastic pursuits, has been constantly carried off by band-boys.

Although no supporting statistics are given, there is no reason to question Brownlow's expression 'full proportion of the prizes'. Brownlow then suggests reasons for this:

The success at school may fairly be attributed to the salutary effect of music upon the character of those boys receiving instruction in the art, which imparts a vivacity to their tempers, and, by its enlivening influence, renders the mental capacities more energetic and susceptible of receiving general instruction, than the faculties of the other boys attain, who do not enjoy the advantage of musical tuition.

(Would that the 'character' of all musicians showed such 'salutary effects' and 'vivacity' of 'temper'!)

The evidence from the Hungarian experiment is the more convincing because of the control exercised. Undoubtedly little boy choristers, and/or their parents, are highly motivated, and to some extent, within the restrictions of competition for entry, self-selected. They usually give the impression of being generally fairly 'bright' to start with. There is no indication as to how Brownlow's foundling band-boys were selected. Furthermore, it is widely observed that the pupils in the State schools who are good at music are usually—not always—good at other subjects. However, it seems that, at least for some children, music education can have beneficial effects outside music.

Then, the following question poses itself: What kind of music education? Let us consider the three examples quoted. (The historian could doubtless provide others.)

Music education on the Kodaly principles is initially vocal, as it was with Curwen in England 100 years ago, before learning to play instruments. From a very early stage, sounds are associated with visual symbols: music reading using solfa, which involves the children in keen listening and thinking about what they are doing.

In the choir schools, again, the basis is singing associated with music reading. Progress in music reading must be rapid in order that these small boys may take part in musically complicated services within a short time of entry. Usually they also learn to play instruments.

In the Foundling Hospital report, only instrumental playing is mentioned but this would also involve music reading, a by no means purely emotional, non-intellectual activity.

It should be noted that the music education of the above three examples, which suggest beneficial effects upon other areas of learning, involves reading, which requires thought, as distinct from idle entertainment. Throughout, at the appropriate level, it is an intellectual challenge. Any education of the emotions—if indeed that is a viable discrete operation—will occur incidentally.

The foregoing in no way denies the emotional appeal of music, which for some people may require no more than the hearing of it. It can appeal to children and adults possessing little or no knowledge and/or skill. Just listening to music, whether in live or recorded performance, has a part to play in music education (see page 16) but with active youngsters it is only a small part. The kind of music education in the three examples described involves much more than an immediate, purely emotional appeal.

Organization and administration of music education

Before further considering what sort of music education in school, it may be useful to consider the circumstances in which it may take place. We are thinking of all children in schools. Let us recall the idea of the sieve (for discovering strengths), and the broad-based triangle. The most important stages are the nursery, infant and junior school. The early years are the time for the widest possible experiences, for acquiring new skills, for the child to discover what interests him and to begin to develop his strengths. Even before the age of 11 years he is developing attitudes, which are the outcome of his interests, strengths and relative weaknesses.

By the time he transfers to secondary school at 11 or 12, he has developed certain attitudes towards music. Those attitudes will depend largely upon the kind of musical experience he has had in the primary school, the kind of teaching, the extent of skill he has gained in music and knowledge about it. Often the attitude is negative because of ignorance—he has *not* been given a chance to come to grips with music in any way comparable with his opportunities in other skills or areas of learning.

The secondary school music teacher often complains about the musical ignorance of the new intake of pupils, not always unjustifiably. But these 11/12 year olds come from several different schools, and hopefully at least a minority are *not* entirely ignorant. Some may sing well and even read music vocally. Some may play the recorder—often very well—and be relatively skilled at reading music instrumentally. A smaller number may have played strings, brass and even woodwind. These latter are usually discovered, or make themselves known, and are soon absorbed into orchestra, band, etc. But recorder players are sometimes ignored in the big secondary school, and similarly the minority of good singers and vocal readers may be lost in the mass.

Ideally, the secondary school staff should know what work has been done in the primary schools: song and other repertoire, music listened to (not just incidentally), vocal reading abilities, instruments played and at what standard. At the least he/she should be able to see the primary teacher's record of work done in class. How often and in what detail is this kept? At best, he would have a record of each individual child's personal musical achievement.

In spite of the problems of record keeping, this can be done, and sometimes is done, even for music, especially in the private sector, when boys and girls are moving from preparatory to public school. 'Personal musical achievement' refers to what John or Mary Smith can do. No one can state what John or Mary can do unless John or Mary have been *tested*. Some kind of achievement tests at the end of the primary school career (as well as intermediate tests earlier, and later on in the secondary school) could stimulate music education in both primary and secondary schools. Reports, or record cards, from primary to secondary school may give information about Reading Age, ability in mathematics, IQ (still used not infrequently!), possibly mention other achievements. Music gets little mention. Expressions such as 'keen', 'not interested', 'plays the violin' or 'recorder' or 'guitar' may be of some general use; but the new teacher needs to know much more, not least what stage in these activities the child has reached. It is impossible to state what stage a child has reached in the absence of criteria against which he can be tested. Hence the need for agreed achievement tests, in which—let us face the fact—some children will do better than others.

The link between primary and secondary schools would doubtless be strengthened if all future music specialist secondary teachers were to spend the first few years of their teaching career in primary schools. Not only would the link be strengthened but it could be advantageous for both teachers and children: the teachers would gain a deeper understanding of children and what they are capable of, musically, at an early age; and the music education of primary school children, and ultimately of secondary school children, should be enhanced.

What about the organization of music in the secondary stage of education? There is probably music in class for all in the first year, usually the equivalent of two periods weekly; and again, *perhaps,* in the second year, by the end of which most pupils will be 13/14 years of age.* From then on I would have no compulsory music in class. All music lessons would be electives—either for continued general interest, or for the inevitably small minority who want to follow music as a study for various examinations, or in small, self-selected groups for singing, any kind of instrumental playing, or listening.

The reasons for this suggestion are twofold:

1. In the interest of the pupil. He may still be interested in music, but by now wants to devote more time and energies to other areas of learning, possibly with an eye on a future career. Or he may just have had enough of music, the kind that is feasible in general class work; and why not? Perhaps we should be more inclined to respect his attitude.

2. In the interest of the teacher. He is, usually, at least at first, an enthusiast. Nothing could be more calculated to kill his enthusiasm than having to face, weekly, the negative and sometimes downright disruptive attitude of some reluctant teenagers. The good musician who is also a good teacher is a rarity; there are not enough to staff all schools. Why waste highly specialized training and skills trying to entertain, often not very successfully, the utterly unwilling, especially when this results in less attention being given to the able and/or at least willing?

Music in the secondary school would not stop at the end of the first or second year. There would be elective classes—for the willing. There would also be—most importantly—choirs, orchestras, bands, listening groups, etc., etc. outside—even better within—the normal timetable. These would consist of the pupils (and staff?) who were not merely having culture thrust upon them, but who were really gaining something

---

* Doubtless music educators would like more time than this; but music is only a part of general education in school. Other areas of learning (subjects) are equally, and in the opinions of many including pupils more, important.

from music, through active participation, or just listening, on a voluntary basis.

These off-the-timetable activities should be regarded as teaching time for the music staff; they cannot indefinitely run extracurricular activities in addition to teaching 30 or 35 class lessons per week. The energy of even the enthusiastic music staff has limits.

Chapter Two

What kind of music in school?

Perhaps this question would be better expressed in the plural: What kinds of music? Even so, to achieve answers that all music educators would agree with is impossible. There must be many reasons for this state of affairs, not the least being the widely varying, sometimes completely revolutionary, experiments of some contemporary composers; and the fact that some music educators are trying to introduce some of these more revolutionary approaches in school.

Let us consider the music education process in school as simply as possible, feasible both from the point of view of the pupil and from that of the teacher. We may do this from the three angles of (1) listener, (2) active participator, as singer or instrumentalist, and (3) creative composer.

Listening, without overt participation, can occur at different levels, from overhearing, or merely being exposed to music, to intense concentration. Even in the concert hall, we can never be sure at which level the listeners are listening; the attention of the most knowledgeable enthusiasts can wander, if only temporarily. In school, the pupils are a captive audience: The timetable states that they will attend the music class on a given day at a given time, whether or not they feel like it; Mr X decides that they shall listen to Bach, Brahms, Britten, Berg or the Beatles. The instrument on which Mr X performs, or the record and reproducing apparatus, may not be in the best condition; and, more likely than not, the seats are hard! In other words, the circumstances are not as propitious as those of the concert hall.

Nevertheless, listening to music of the kind that neither the teacher nor the children can perform themselves is an important, if not, in terms of time, a major part of music education. Without it children would be deprived of the opportunity of gaining musical experience and knowledge that may indeed give them pleasure at the time or arouse an interest that may survive into later life. In this respect at least the child of the late 20th century is at an advantage over his predecessor of 100 years ago.

What is played, and what the children hear, depends largely upon the individual preference of the teacher. He may also sometimes allow the pupils to play recorded items of their own choice; but until they have acquired some small repertoire they have nothing to choose from.

This raises the question: What shall they listen to? It may range from Palestrina, or earlier, to the latest pop; from the lutenists to the most recent electronic experiments. One must hope that whatever is played has some genuine musical interest and that attention is drawn to this. One also hopes that the teacher's personal preferences for music of a particular composer, period or style do not restrict his choice unduly. If children are to acquire knowledge of musical styles, they must have the opportunity to hear a wide range of styles.

Furthermore, no one can know a piece of music on a single hearing. Therefore whatever is chosen should contain sufficient musical interest to bear enough repetition for children to become really familiar with it, to be able to remember and, on a subsequent occasion, recognize it. Again, whatever the length of the piece, and however much attention may earlier have been drawn to important features of it, at some stage time should be found for them to hear it whole, from beginning to end. We are dealing with a work of art, long or short, old or modern, popular or classical. Merely to be presented with bits of it, however interesting in themselves, and never to hear it whole, is aesthetically unsatisfying.

One must assume that the teacher has chosen a piece of music because he wants the children to know it, to remember it for future reference, in addition to any immediate pleasurable satisfaction a first hearing may give; and of the pleasure factor we can never be sure, as has been suggested earlier. Memory depends upon quality of attention and repetition. How often must an individual hear (listen to) a piece of music in order to remember enough of it to be able at least to recognize it later? We do not know the answer. It must vary from individual to individual, and to some extent depend upon clues of association that are not necessarily musical in themselves.

Such clues may be associated with the particular circumstances of the first hearing. A second hearing may recall those particular circumstances; or recall of the circumstances may trigger off memory of the music. It may be a particular aria at the opera, a motet sung in a cathedral, hearing some other person's record, incidental music in the cinema, something heard on the radio or television. It may be something heard in school. The list of examples of association is endless. Recording companies thrive on it. The obvious implication is that when one has heard something that caught the attention, one wants to hear it again. This should not be overlooked; in their quite estimable desire to give yet wider experience and knowledge in the limited time available, teachers in school sometimes do overlook this important fact.

Sufficient repetition as an essential for remembering music, coupled with the possibility of the influence of non-musical association, was indicated in a recent rather lighthearted experiment with children between the ages of 4 and 11 years. (Thackray, R. M. 1974).

Twenty short extracts from signature tunes of popular television programmes were recorded on tape, excluding all verbal clues, and played to some 4 year-olds in a nursery school. They easily identified all the tunes, usually very quickly; also enthusiastically. This prompted an extension of the experiment to 386 older children, aged 9 to 11 years, in several schools. Of these 386, only 6 children did not see television regularly, and as a result knew few of the tunes. With the remaining 380, the mean score was 19 out of a possible 20. (These obviously did spend considerable time watching TV). Again, as with the much younger children, identification was almost instantaneous as well as accurate.

Presumably children who watched these programmes regularly had heard the tunes many times (how many it is impossible to say), and they firmly associated them with essentially non-musical circumstances. (Only one of the twenty programmes which the signature tunes introduced was concerned with 'music': *Top of the Pops!*)

Repeated hearing of these tunes was obviously an important factor in the memorizing of them, even though the quality of the listening was not likely to be of the kind used by the keen, musical, concert-goer. Rather is it more likely that it was nearer to overhearing, with little fully-conscious attention to the music itself.

It supports the observation that children's ability to memorize and identify music seems to develop naturally and spontaneously, and is independent of reading and playing ability. Of course, for identification, as distinct from memory for the music itself, clues must be given, whether they are the titles of TV programmes, or the title of a piece. As clues to identification, *Jackanory* or *Tomorrow's World* are just as valid as *Kreutzer Sonata* or *Beethoven Sonata for Violin and Pianoforte in A op.* 47.

This apparent ease with which children memorize music is of great advantage to both children and teacher. Without verbalization, apart from clues for identification, children can become acquainted with, get to know, learn, a great deal of music, through listening, or merely hearing, only.

This is also the way in which very young children learn a vocal repertoire. Their teachers sing or play nursery rhymes, and other songs, and soon the children are also singing what they have heard. Admittedly words of songs may assist melodic memorization, but they are not essential to memorization of the musical element; the experiment with TV signature tunes alone is evidence of this.

In conjunction with bodily movements that are more obvious than those involved in singing, this is also the way many children begin to play instruments; but the 'tune' must be in their heads, otherwise their body movements would result in inaccurate performance.

The advantage of this early memorization of music may also be a considerable disadvantage in music education. Children and their teachers may rely on it too much; sometimes apparently almost exclusively. As a result, the reading of visual symbols representing sounds is neglected. The result is that, improvisation apart, the child is left permanently in the state when he cannot explore for himself music already composed. He can never read the book: Always the story must be read, or told, to him.

Easy memorization, without skill in reading music, makes it possible for children to become acquainted with a quite large repertoire of music during their school life. Apart from listening in class, they can also hear music in assembly, and at occasional concerts in school. How much information is given about the music, the composer, or the circumstances in which it was written, must be decided by the teacher, who knows the children. But two things should never be overlooked: (1) a piece of music should be repeated sufficiently often for the children to become reasonably well acquainted with it, i.e. to remember at least a good deal of it; (2) a clue for identification of the piece should always be given for future reference, preferably title, if any, and name of composer; plus as much additional information as the teacher considers appropriate.

If a live performance is given by teacher or pupils, in class or assembly, it must be well done. Children quickly sense incompetence. It is worth remembering that the simple piece beautifully played rarely fails to make impact.

Earlier it was suggested that, although, important, listening to music that the children cannot themselves perform was not a major part of music education, that is in terms of proportional time. Much else needs to be fitted into the limited time available. Furthermore, music itself takes time; it can exist only in terms of timespan. A picture, or piece of statuary, may be perceived whole in a matter of seconds; although one may wish to spend more time examining detail. A given span of time is not of the essence of such perception. In music, time *is* of the essence. Even the expert reader of a simple score cannot form a true impression in less time than it would take to perform the piece.

To make optimum use of the limited time he can allocate to listening only, the teacher must make choices of what shall be heard. This responsibility cannot be avoided. He may take the view that only contemporary music is relevant to today's children and choose accordingly. On the other hand I suspect that most music educators would subscribe to the viewpoint that it was their responsibility to acquaint pupils with some of the more notable compositions of various periods of the past, as well as those of the present. In literature we acquaint our pupils with some of the work of great authors of the past. (Or do we?) If we do not do something comparable in music, might we not be found guilty of causing positive deprivation?

One further thought about the circumstances of listening. When attending a live performance, one does not close one's eyes for the duration. Vision, the sight of the performers, adds interest and, despite the distraction of the antics of some of the more athletic conductors, probably aids concentration. Recorded music, even live performance on the radio, however closely approximating to the live performance in sound, is at most a second best: the performers are not present. Fortunately videotape and the necessary equipment are becoming more accessible. As Percy Scholes and others welcomed the gramophone into education almost half a century ago, so perhaps we may now look forward to recorded vision as well as sound in the schoolroom. It would still not be the live performance, but vision would bring the approximation one stage nearer to reality.

It will be noted, I hope, that in this section on listening I have not mentioned the word appreciation. What I have been writing about is simply becoming acquainted with, getting to know, some music, that the children cannot perform themselves. A comprehensive music education must surely include this aspect.

Active participation—recreative and creative

Most of the time children do not want to sit still and listen. They want to be doing something, and that involves some kind of physical movement. When they hear music, very young children often move or 'dance' to it, or join in vocally, unprompted by adults. When the music has a strong metrical pulse they will sometimes join in 'instrumentally', using any sound-producing material that is at hand, e.g. spoons, rattles or sticks. Since music is movement of sound in time, it is not unnatural that children should indulge in active participation. Thus for most of the time music education is devoted to active participation: singing, moving to music, playing instruments. The hundreds of books and courses on music education concentrate mainly on achieving this.

Singing

In spite of the proliferation of classroom and other instruments in schools, singing is still the most important medium for music education. The voice is the most intimately controlled, and, well used, the most beautiful of musical instruments. It is the most easily portable, and, incidentally, the cheapest. If all our other instruments were taken away there could still be music.

The child walking along the noisy city street quietly singing to herself is making music, just as is the professional choir singing motets or madrigals. A century ago, as mentioned earlier, most music education in schools was restricted to singing. One unfortunate result of the advent, in the last fifty years, of recorded music and classroom instruments is the relative neglect of singing. Yet one of our most distinguished string players could tell a group of instrumental teachers 'unless you can sing, at least inside you, you cannot play!'

Although singing has been comparatively neglected in recent years, one may still hear beautiful singing by young children in some primary schools, and a few secondary schools produce choirs of very high standards. In these cases the pupils have been shown how to use their voices to produce the desired choral effects. Vocal training, or voice training—old-fashioned as that expression may be—is still important if good results are to be achieved. From the point of view of the pupils taking part there can be great personal satisfaction. Such satisfaction can happen even in the singing of a whole school at assembly.

Apart from some knowledge of how to help children to sing with a pleasing tone, perhaps the most important consideration is the choice of what to sing. To some extent this is a subjective operation, and may also be influenced by current fashion; but there is no need to try to court popularity by choosing only songs that are in a 'pop' idiom, or have a West Indian or any other particular national 'flavour', or are accompanied by guitar. There is nothing wrong with any of these but they should not be the sole fare. It is also worth mentioning that boys do not always prefer songs that are loud and jolly any more than girls always prefer songs that are sweet and low.

Words will also influence the choice of songs; but the chief limitation on choice is a musical one: the vocal range and tessitura of an item. The melodic line(s) should lie within the fairly easy range of the children's present stage of vocal development and training (see Cleall and Joyner). That certainly is a limitation, but a very wide one, for within it there exists an enormous amount of vocal music of high quality that will stand the frequent repetition necessary for memorization.

Instrument playing: percussion instruments

Probably the most obvious development in music education during the last 25 years has been the enormous increase in instrumental playing in both primary and secondary schools. Prior to about 1950 there were instrumental groups in some schools, but rarely full orchestras. There was a little recorder playing, and a number of 'Percussion Bands' normally composed of non-pitch-change instruments: small traingles, drums, cymbals, etc.

Since about 1950 there has been a huge increase in recorder playing, in the playing of orchestral instruments (strings, woodwind, brass) leading to some individual schools having full symphony orchestras and brass and other wind ensembles; and in so-called classroom instruments, most usually pitch percussion instruments such as glocken-spiels, xylophones, chime-bars, etc. A distinction must be made between the last mentioned group and the former: The former, the orchestral instruments, require considerable skill involving much practice and determination to surmount technical difficulties; the latter, the percussion instruments, produce instant, quite pleasant sounding, results, requiring comparatively little skill. (I am thinking of what goes on in school, as distinct from orchestral percussion playing which requires certain types of skills of a very high order. Conceivably the development of such skills could take place in the classroom; in practice, it rarely does.)

The timbre of the instruments generally used is not harsh even when played fairly loudly. It is usually pleasing, even if to some listeners it soon becomes tedious. Because of their tonal quality, even simultaneously sounded semitones have a much less striking dissonant and disturbing effect than such semitones played on the keyboard or on pairs of orchestral instruments or recorders. When only the bars required for the pentatonic scale are used, with the semitones removed, there is negligible strident effect of dissonance and disturbance. This is splendid, for a limited period of experience, at any age. Children can discover much for themselves about different qualities of sounds produced by the different instruments, and through different ways of playing the same instrument. They can learn to play melodies they already know, or devise their own. They can discover how to combine different melodies in a way that gives them satisfaction. They can learn something about chords (groups of sounds played simultaneously). They can go further and create their own concerted items. A knowledgeable and stimulating teacher can lead them on to even more musical adventures.

The pupils have to use at least three of their senses: hearing, vision and touch.* The more of the five senses involved, the more the learning process ought to be 'enriched', even if the movements are, relatively to those required in other instrumental playing, somewhat gross. Experience with these instruments should assist the development of the sense of relative pitch, timbre, degrees of loudness and duration (within small limits); all these are ingredients of music. Their immediate availability, and the fact that the playing of them requires relatively little skill, can result in temporarily fairly satisfying performances by most children. They can stimulate the imagination and provide easy means for these children to create their own pieces of music. It is maintained that they can assist children to read music; this cannot be denied, but there may be quicker and more efficient ways.

Yet their novelty (when children first meet them), ease of manipulation, and instant results can also bear the seeds of disadvantage for wider music education. Apart from the immediate 'fun', where does it lead?

---

* The 'vision' here referred to is that of looking at the instrument, not at music notation or other printed symbols; that activity may, or may not, come later. In terms of kinaesthetic movement in association with memory for spatial distances, this activity cannot be compared with, for example, keyboard playing where the keys (notes) are much closer together and played not with a beater but directly with the fingers, thus requiring much finer control.

One has to be constantly reminded that time is limited in the school day and percussion sessions can be extremely time consuming. One result of this has been that, in many schools, singing has been neglected since these instruments became more easily available. Another is that, after the initial excitement of novelty, their sound, admittedly varied but only within limits, can become tedious.*

For the majority of children who are unlikely to play 'conventional' instruments, these percussion instruments provide an experience of instrumental participation that would otherwise be missed. That is good. But it is within a very restricted area of the totality of musical experience. Even in terms of bodily movement it bears little resemblance to that needed for more 'conventional' instrumental playing.† Again for the majority, other musical experiences, especially singing and listening, should not be neglected. For the minority who possess greater aptitude for music, it is most important that their latent abilities be discovered early and developed as far as their potential allows. This leads to consideration of the playing of instruments requiring more intricate skills.

Other instruments

As distinct from the pitch and non-pitch percussion instruments, all stringed (including the guitar), wind (including the recorder) and even

---

* In the *Times Educational Supplement* of 26 July 1974 (p.12) Robin Maconie (1974) reviewing a national festival, stated: 'I can think of no more purgatorial experience than a concert of chime bars, glockenspiels and harmonicons'. Strongly subjective no doubt; but he is not alone, and in his company there may be many children, especially the more musically sensitive.

† It was interesting to observe some children performing in the Royal Festival Hall, London. The group consisted of a few violin players, a few recorder players and a few pitch-percussion players. The string and recorder players played consistently on the conductor's beat. The pitch-percussion players were almost equally consistently behind the beat and even within their own sub-group their ensemble was ragged. I suggest that the different kinds of manipulative movements involved might have been responsible for this: the finer and more intimate movements of the string and recorder players being under more direct control of the cortex than those of the percussion players with their beaters. Associated with this, the violin and recorder players could feel with their fingers for their note positions whilst watching the conductor: The percussion players had to spend much more time looking at their instruments in order to direct their beaters to the correct location amongst the bars. It may be noted that all these children were playing by rote: The reading of printed notation was not involved in the performance, thus avoiding a further distraction.

keyboard instruments are played in more intimate contact with the body, and are thus under finer and more delicate control. They also require skills of a higher order.

The recorder

Of these instruments, probably the most extensively played by young children is the recorder. The descant recorder is small enough for the fingers of most 7 year-old children. The playing of it, like that of all other wind instruments, is intimately associated with the body and singing. Breath, the mouth and fingers are all used at the same time; plus of course the monitoring of the ears which applies to all forms of music making. The recorder provided thousands of children with their first experience of instrumental playing before pitch percussion instruments became widely available; it is still extensively used.

Whereas children can be, and sometimes are, 'turned loose' on class-room pitch percussion instruments, encouraged to experiment, even 'create' with them, skills of recorder playing must be taught and learnt correctly from the beginning. This involves teacher direction, and application on the part of the children. Incorrect manipulation can lead to bad playing habits, and these, once formed, are difficult to eradicate. Thus the teaching of, and learning to play, the recorder inevitably involves formal instruction, however currently unpopular that may be to some educationists. Merely to give children recorders and tell them to experiment, would result not only in bad playing habits, but in some extremely nasty noises, intolerable to at least the more aurally sensitive children. Few teachers, however informal their approach in other activities, would do this, if only out of sheer self-preservation!

This gives rise to other remarks on teaching the recorder in class, or in groups of more than five or six. In the first place, the recorder is essentially a solo, not a union chorus, instrument. It is easier to play in tune, or more accurately 'almost in tune', than some other wind instruments. But two or more descant recorders played at the unison can be so nearly in tune but yet not quite there that the aural result is quite distressing. This could be a reason why some children dislike it. The players must have a keen sense of pitch discrimination and listen intently all the time. This applies when two or only very few players are involved. When attempts are made to teach whole classes of 25, 30 or more children, the results are musically excruciating.

Apart from the slight out-of-tune-ness on the same note, wrong fingering on the part of some children results in further confounding the situation with wrong notes. A teacher cannot all the time be watching every child's fingering for every note in such large groups.

So despite all its advantages in introducing children to instrumental playing, and often incidentally to music reading, I suggest that recorder playing as a whole class activity may do as much harm as good, and that it should never be taught to more than very small groups at a time. Thus the teacher can see what every child is doing, and pay attention to the musical potentialities of the instrument.

The same applies, and is usually practised, in the teaching of all other wind and string instruments; but as these are bigger, more expensive and not so easily available as the descant recorder, the temptation to indulge in teaching impossibly large groups does not exist.

Orchestral instruments

We now turn to the playing of orchestral instruments. It is in this activity that the most remarkable development has taken place in the last quarter century. Mention of the National Youth Orchestra, the British Youth Symphony Orchestra, the National Youth Brass Band, many other county, city, town and even individual school orchestras, brings to mind standards of playing that are near-professional.* These have been achieved through increased technical proficiency and sensitivity, leading, one hopes, to greater musical understanding. This, in turn, brings additional personal satisfaction and fulfilment to the pupils involved, a 'difference' for the better, a valid educational objective.

Another important aspect of this is the social one: individuals working co-operatively as a team, making their own maximum effort but at the same time submitting their own individualities to the direction of a conductor or section leader. Without such discipline no music ensemble

---

* 'Youth orchestras are a phenomenon of our times; previous centuries did not see their like. Today's youth orchestras are of amazing virtuosity and dedication. Whenever any of my conductor friends bemoan the future fate of the symphony orchestra. I renew my faith by thinking of the equation that a 20th-century youth orchestra will mean a 21st-century professional orchestra.' (André Previn, 1974, p.9.)

could operate, excepting the circumstances of a very few avant-garde experiments.*

We may ask how this development in instrumental playing has come about. We may also ask what proportion of the total number of school pupils actually participates? And what happens to the rest?

How it came about. Obviously private tuition, outside school, makes an important contribution. In school, the contribution has been made principally through small group tuition given by instrumental experts working as peripatetic teachers. The teaching of string playing in small groups became more and more widespread from the late 1940s and early 1950s, thanks largely to the tireless inspiration of Mr Bernard Shore, the Staff Inspector for Music of the time, and Miss Gertrude Collins. Small group instruction in wind playing followed. In many parts of the country, this work in the schools has been further comple-mented by the establishment of area Junior Music Schools, usually held on Saturdays. Thus, from quite early stages in technical competence, children had increasing opportunity to play, not only in the individual lesson but also in small group lessons, and in the bigger combinations of elementary, intermediate and senior orchestras and bands: a personally satisfying operation. The most able and diligent can reach the local and national orchestras and bands.

Again the simile of the sieve or the triangle (see p. 14 above) is applicable: a broad base leading towards an apex. Many of those who start on instrumental tuition may not progress beyond the elementary stage, fewer will reach and stop at an intermediate stage, and fewer still will reach the senior stage. Those who go beyond that may be only a tiny majority of those who began. How far they go depends on a combination of ability and attitude; but at least many more children now have the opportunity than was the case a quarter of a century ago.

What happens in private tuition and in the small group instruction in school is quite different from the kind of operation with classroom

---

* Not everyone would agree. For example, Schafer, 1973, p.3 in an article entitled 'Where does it all lead?' colourfully criticizes the whole idea of orchestras and choirs:
   '. . . the orchestra or band, in which one man rides herd over sixty or a hundred others, is at best aristocratic, and more frequently dictatorial. Or what about the choir in which a heterogenous (sic) collection of voices is brought together in such a way that no single voice is permitted to assert itself above the homogeneous "blend" of the group? Choral singing is the most beautiful example of communism ever achieved by man.'
   On this kind of statement the reader must form his own opinion.

percussion instruments mentioned earlier. It may still be fun, or play, but, for however long it lasts, it is serious play, for both teacher and pupils. Whatever the methods used, the objective is to learn to play particular instruments as well as possible. This is achieved by getting stuck into the basic techniques of playing the chosen instrument. Usually before long, if not at the beginning, association of what is being played with the visual symbols of music notation is involved. Progress, and the personal satisfaction that comes from it, requires concentration, practice, determination, and even hard work—features that are all too often absent from general music classes. No amount of mere unguided experimenting in so-called 'learning situations' or 'creativity' will help a child to 'discover' how to play *well* on a violin, oboe or trumpet any more than it would on the recorder.

Teachers of instruments, whether on full-time appointment in one school, or peripatetic visiting a number of schools, are employed because they are themselves competent players, and, we hope, have studied something of the art and techniques of teaching children. Furthermore, allowing for some inevitable so-called wastage, they are expected to produce results: That at least a fair proportion of their pupils will achieve the satisfaction of making some progress in their playing; and that means progress in at least one important aspect of music education.

One can only guess an answer to the question about the proportion of the total number of school pupils who actually participate in instrumental playing. There must be some who play for instance the currently popular guitar, or other instruments, entirely apart from school. Even when we restrict the question to those who have school-based tuition, we can do little more than estimate the proportion except to agree that it is not large.

Perhaps we may get some indication from a recent unpublished survey, made by a research student, in a large county that makes quite generous provision for instrumental teaching in its schools. This calculated that about 6 per cent of the school population was learning to play instruments (excluding the recorder). Other counties may achieve higher or lower proportions. If reliable figures are available on a national basis I am not aware of them. However I would imagine that, again excluding the recorder, not more than about 10 per cent of school children are learning to play an instrument. That leaves about 90 per cent having to depend entirely for their music education on what they get in general class work.

Again, one can only guess at the reasons for this. They may include a shortage of specialist instrumental teachers and a shortage of available instruments; also lack of inclination or interest or abilities on the part of the pupils, reflecting attitudes (again) possibly arising from lack of early experience in music and early training in basic skills. There are doubtless other reasons.

However, for the minority who do have instrumental tuition, their music education and their general education have been so much more variegated and enhanced through the added dimension of instrumental training.

One reservation should be made. Instrumental playing alone is not the whole of music education. There is one unfortunate aspect of sole, or almost entire, reliance on it. Many technically advanced and sensitive instrumental players are musical cripples without the aid of their instruments; ask them to sing, or whistle, a simple melody at sight and they are helpless. These people seem to have come to regard the visual symbols of notation as instructions to manipulate, and to rely upon their instruments to do their tonal thinking for them. This could be described as a side effect of concentration on instrumental music making. I would call it a central defect. It would not have happened in the elementary schools of about a century ago; neither, of course, would the instrumental work.

Progress involves change, but the reverse is not necessarily true. Ability to hear in the head the line(s) of the printed score is essential for the singer who does not learn everything secondhand and by rote. It is also highly desirable for the instrumentalist. The only ways in which he can demonstrate this ability are by either singing or whistling the sounds indicated by the notation, or by indicating orally or in writing when errors are made, sometimes by himself, more usually by another person. There is no reason why the dexterous manipulator of instruments should not be helped additionally to hear the notes in his head; this is something that can be done in school in the general music class, and the earlier the better.

There is another aspect to instrumental playing that is not often mentioned. It could be that the satisfaction obtained from playing an instrument is fundamentally physical (kinaesthetic), with a secondary satisfaction in the sounds produced as a result of manipulation of the instrument. Or the two satisfactions may be equal, even allowing for some ungratifying sounds emitted in the early stages of learning to play some instruments! As musicians and teachers, are we always aware of this particular kind of physical satisfaction, of sheer physical challenge in music practice? For evidence of such satisfaction (to himself if to no one else) watch a small child playing a drum. At the other extreme consider the more advanced player of, for instance, the oboe (a monodic instrument), or of the organ (a polyphonic instrument involving 'pedipulation' as well as 'manipulation'). The challenge is physical: The eye scans the score, the brain activates the limbs. It is only when the physical movements have been made in contact with the instrument that the ear, which is not a scanner like the eye but only a receiver, becomes involved as referee. In practising more and more difficult studies (études) we are submitting ourselves to further physical challenges; we are developing our neuro-muscular skills in a way not dissimilar to that involved in developing comparable motor skills in games, in tightrope walking, in typing. A good thing to do and physically satisfying; but let us be clear about the processes. It is the satisfaction of making bodily movements in order to produce sounds from an instrument that, unlike the voice, is external to the body itself.

Recent electronic devices for the creation of music are even further removed from the body than conventional instruments. (I do not refer here to such instruments as electronic organs). Doubtless new physical satisfactions will be increasingly derived from creating sounds on synthesizers, tape recorders, and the like, and manipulating these in playback. But this is still at a relatively experimental stage, like much of the new music that has been composed and performed in the last twenty years.

Creativity—composition

We have discussed musical experience from the angles of listener and active participator (chiefly as re-creator). The third angle, that of creative composer, has been merely hinted at. Most singing and instrumental playing is re-creative of music already composed, usually, by someone other than the re-creator. But in every performance there must be a creative element if it is to convey, through the interpretation by the performer, a musical message to the listener.

Now, briefly, we shall consider the creator, the composer. Of all the hundreds of really first rate executants, very few indeed are also composers. Many composers do not claim to be first rate performers.

Of the many thousands of music graduates who have demonstrated knowledge of the tools of composition in their 'exercises', some of them of considerable proportions, few have had their works performed, except perhaps as part of their degree courses and examinations; even fewer continue to compose.

The reasons for this state of affairs are elusive. The skills of being able to put musical ideas together in a coherent composition for a degree 'exercise' are acknowledged in the award of the degree. The candidate has learnt the craft. But something more is required of the composer who is to be accepted as such; and of the many 'craftsmen', few become accepted composers.

Then there are the high-ranking performers who do not compose. They spend their professional lives performing at the highest level music of a generally accepted high quality and interest. One reason why they do not compose may be lack of time: They are so busy performing, and maintaining their high standards that they have no time to compose music. Another reason may be that every performance is an act not only of re-creation, but also of creation. The composer has provided his score, his instructions, his recipe, for the artiste to bring the music to life in performance. No two performances of a given work are identical and the differences of interpretation are an indication of the element of creativity in re-creation. The composer notates his original ideas, the performer creates the actual sounds. From their separate functions each may derive comparable satisfaction.

This is, of course, specualtion because we have no means of measuring objectively the degrees or quality of those satisafactions. Nevertheless, since there are so many first rate performers who do not compose, it would seem that interpretive performance is wholly rewarding, intellectually, aesthetically, emotionally.

A similar situation applies at less exalted levels. Children in school, judging by their appearance, and on their own evidence (we cannot measure this objectively), can derive great personal satisfaction from working hard upon, and then performing, music composed by others. They may also try composing their own music, and this may bring its own particular satisfaction, but it is a different kind of satisfaction from performance of music, however simple or complicated, by accepted masters of composition. Furthermore composition whether notated or tape recorded is time-consuming, and whilst it may be encouraged, in my view it should not be at the total expense of getting to know some of the acknowledged 'masterpieces' through either performance or listening. I state this belief because I think that something worthwhile rubs off through contact with great (not necessarily long) pieces of musical art. This is not perhaps the most popular view amongst some contemporary music educators, but it is one that is held by not a few, and one which therefore should be stated.

Sometimes the view is expressed that we have far more performers than composers because of the educational system which, it is claimed, inhibits self-expression; which deals only, or mainly, with music of the past—a sort of museum culture. The time taken in achieving the mere fluency of writing notes on paper, let alone studying, and trying to write like, former (but not necessarily dead as yet!) composers, was arduous and inhibiting. Now, in the last quarter century, all is changed by the tape recorder. We can 'think aloud' into the microphone and, lo, our 'creative' thoughts are recorded for all (who choose) to hear. All is spontaneity. Gone is the tedium. At last we have instant composition.* Yet, since so few of the many acknowledged first-rate musicians themselves compose, or possibly even feel the urge to compose, is it realistic to expect all children, or even most, to exhibit original creative ability in music? Is the considerable time currently devoted to this operation by some enthusiasts, with resulting loss of time for re-creative activity (which it has been suggested, in music peculiarly amongst the arts, contains a creative element) making the optimum use of our pupils' time?

To the last question some answers will be in the affirmative, if only for the reason that children are more likely to understand music, and the composition of it, when they themselves have attempted to compose it. This is true, up to a point; the activity is even desirable as a small part of music education (and in fact is by no means new†), but not to the exclusion of other equally, or even more, important parts.

The fact remains that, just as it is possible to know (which includes memory for) a great deal of music through listening only, without ability to read a score or perform, so it is possible to be a performer of the highest order without composing music. Of the totality of musicians the composers is a rare phenomenon.

There is a sufficiently vast, rich repertoire of music, from the last six or seven centuries including the 20th, of occidental culture alone,

---

* '. . . now . . . there is no longer a craft of composition to learn. But music has not so far benefited from the disappearance of a discipline which at least provided an elementary yardstick by which to judge musical talent, *and made it possible to identify incompetence.*' (Cooper, 1969, p.15.)

† cf for example Sir Walford Davies's work on the radio in the 1930s, Lucy M. Welch, 1933, p.7, *et al.*

to satisfy most musicians most of the time, and to provide material for listening and recreative performance in education.

Whilst children should certainly be encouraged to create their own original music, and be given the means to do this—remembering that they already have the voice as a creative instrument—genuine creative originality is likely to be as rare in school as in the world of music at large. Spending an inordinate amount of time on trying to develop original creativity must result in an unbalanced music education and the neglect of what for most children, and adults, would be musically more worthwhile.

Chapter Three

Music for every child?

What happens to the rest of the children who do not sing in special groups or play orchestral instruments? This is the approximately 90 per cent who, for their music education, must rely on what they experience in the general music class. The question has been raised earlier but not answered.

'Music for every child and every child for music' sounds fine as a slogan, but what exactly does it mean? For example, does it mean *every* child up to the age of 18 or 19 years? Must every child, pupil, student—call him what we will—have regular compulsory music classes in school, or have provision made for any and every kind of possible musical activity according to his developing or changing interests in, and attitude towards, music? In spite of negative attitudes that may have developed in adolescence, is the implication that he must, nevertheless, spend some part of every week in school 'doing' some kind of music—regular doses of some form of musical culture, whether listening to Bach or instant creativity?

Such an interpretation of the slogan is unrealistic. Firstly, it ignores the developing and changing attitudes of pupils as they grow older. Secondly, there are not enough music educators to cope with such demands. Thirdly, there do not exist enough accommodation, instruments and other equipment; and the cost of providing such would be so exorbitant as to be unacceptable to those who provide the finances: That is the public at large, taxpayers and ratepayers including parents. Fourthly, even if such facilities and equipment could be provided for every child, it is extremely unlikely that it would be put to anything approaching optimum use; already there must be many thousands of pounds worth of such equipment in the schools of the country, bought in an initial flush of enthusiasm and now stored away in cupboards or odd corners, rarely if ever used. The economic factor in education is by no means unimportant.

I would re-write the slogan less tersely, but, bearing in mind the facts of life, more realistically, as follows:

From an early age as wide experience of music as possible, in class and outside it, for all children up to about 12 or 13 years of age, and from then on for as long as they show some interest.

Reasons for this viewpoint have already been indicated.

This implies regular class work in music for all up to about 12 or 13 years of age, plus additional opportunities of choral singing, and instrumental playing on a voluntary, self- or teacher-selected basis. This happens in numerous primary schools; but even at this early age it is universally observed that by no means all children opt for these additional experiences however stimulating the class work may be.

Leaving aside such additional experiences, what happens, or can happen, in the compulsorily attended classroom work? In the English educational system, for which there is no nationally prescribed syllabus, the variety of music education is enormous and there can be no single answer. All I can do is to indicate what I know happens in some schools, and to suggest what I think could, and even should, happen, given competent teachers.

I shall try to reduce this to simple fundamental terms, with the following principle in mind: Class work, however stimulating and immediately enjoyable (which we hope it is), is education, which is more than mere entertainment. It should lay sound musical foundations for, and have relevance to, those children who also opt for additional choral and instrumental experience. Whilst inevitably catering for the majority, it must not neglect the minority. Whilst maintaining the interest of the majority, it should also form a broad basis of music education that is pertinent to the minority of instrumental players.

Thus the general class work for all will include:

1. Getting to know a wide range of music through listening only.
2. Singing a wide variety of vocal music appropriate to the age, and possibly sex, of the pupils. This would also include some training in how to use the voice.
3. Some playing of 'classroom' instruments, not only for 'creative' purposes, and not only for 'avant garde' type sounds.

4. Learning to read, and write, the currently conventional (i.e. most widely used) visual symbols for sounds: staff notation.

These four activities I propose as fundamental to music *education,* and all children should at least be given opportunity to take part in them. Experience in all of them can start from a very early age in the infant school.

The ideas are not new; neither is most of the music we daily encounter. They are not dull activities in the hands of a competent, interesting and imaginative teacher. (The opposite kind of teacher would fail to arouse interest in any area of learning.) They present a challenge to the children and demand of them some effort: These features in themselves are some insurance against the activities becoming intrinsically dull. They are not unrealistic suggestions if the teaching is competent: All occur in some primary schools and in the 11 to 13 age range in some secondary schools. They are not restrictive, and they can be implemented with a variety of different methods.

Their adoption could at least give a sense of direction to music education at a time when, in the welter of new ideas being proposed in some quarters, such a sense of direction is lacking.

The first three types of activity are fairly commonly employed in many schools. The fourth, music reading, tends to be neglected at the present time.* Because of this neglect of reading, I propose to discuss the matter a little further; also because I maintain that music reading, preferably vocal, is the surest foundation for sound music education, however currently neglected the notion may be.

Music reading

Listening to music does not require the ability to read notation; neither does the singing of a melody heard often enough to remember it; neither, again, does the playing of an instrument essentially demand reading ability: It can be learnt by direct imitation. When so much musical knowledge and satisfaction can be gained without it, why bother to teach reading?

* In a survey (Reading University/Schools Council project) conducted in 1971 in 133 primary schools in several parts of England, teachers were asked to place in rank order of importance six aspects of class music. They came out in the following order (most important at the top, least at the bottom):

1.	Singing	4.	Listening
2.	Instrumental work	5.	Music and movement
3.	Creative work	6.	Music reading

No reasons for this rank order were given; they can only be surmised.

Music reading and writing is not even important, as is language reading and writing, for communication of one's basic needs. It is only concerned with music, which in itself is 'useless' (see above). Equally useless, it may be maintained, are some other skills and knowledge learnt in school; if we acted upon all the different cries for 'relevance to contemporary living' in education, there might be little left to teach and learn.

However, the child who cannot read language must always have the story read to him. He is utterly dependent on person-to-person contact. Literature, even the popular press, is denied to him. (Admittedly there are illiterate adults who contrive to survive even in our highly complex society.) Furthermore, education is generally conceived as something more than the mere learning to survive.

As the person who cannot read is deprived of coming to grips with any form of literature for himself, so is the person who cannot read music deprived of active participation in any music that he has not memorized by listening to others. The musically illiterate member of a choral group has to depend on those around him; the instrumentalist is at an even greater disadvantage.

I have also proposed that general class music should lay sound musical foundations for, and have relevance to, those children who also opt for additional choral and instrumental experience (p. 46 above); and some ability to read can open doors for the rest. What is more, children can be taught to read music in class, can enjoy the operation, and can gain much satisfaction from the fact that reading enables them to perform more music than they could do otherwise.

Concerning music reading in the primary school, the Plowden Report (1967) states (para. 692 (c)):

The importance of musical literacy is not fully understood. Without it, independent effort, progression and discovery are impossible, and unfamiliarity with musical notation breeds the kind of suspicion that verbal illiteracy usually brings in its train. Some teachers believe that learning to read music increases difficulties and diminishes enjoyment, whereas the contrary is true.

At least one teacher apparently believes that the 'difficulties' (of the last sentence above) are not the only matter for concern. In replying to an examination question about music reading this person wrote:

I feel there is almost a 'class' element in notation. By and large, music in working class society means playing *without* (written) music, and in middle class society means playing *with* music—in both cases exclusively.

How many members of choral societies and amateur orchestras are 'working class'? What about the players in brass bands, some of whose performances are of the highest professional standards? Are all professional orchestral players 'middle class'? In terms of financial rewards, relative to those of some 'working class' employees in industry, many are 'working-class' and hard-working at that! How sociologically crazy can we be?

It is not unworthy of note that in the English Board Schools of a century ago, despite limitations of equipment and general facilities, 'working class' children were taught to read music, i.e. sing from visual symbols, whether Curwen's solfa symbolization or staff notation. This was during the few decades of 'payment by results'. If the children in a school could sing a certain number of songs by rote the grant to the school was sixpence per child; if they could also read music (sing at sight) this grant was doubled. Human nature being what it is, School Boards and teachers ensured that children could sing, and read music; and the teacher training colleges ensured that their students could teach children to read! The 'payment by results' system lapsed, and so, eventually, did the ability of most children to read music.

Whether all this was a 'good thing' or not I am not sure. Certain it is, however, that under this system choral societies flourished in cities, towns and smaller communities. Only a minority played instruments but vast numbers sang, and furthermore sang via an intelligent comprehension of the printed symbols of music.

John Curwen and Sarah Glover were largely responsible for this development of widespread music reading via the voice. Through the Tonic Solfa System, the germs of which had a long, varied and respectable history, they promulgated an easily comprehensible introduction to the reading of music without the need of instruments which require manipulation and which, at the time, were expensive. Nothing more was needed than human voices, some means of reference to pitch (tuning fork or pitch pipe carried in the pocket), chalk board and possibly a pitch chart normally referred to as a modulator.

Helmholtz was amazed to hear 40 children (ages 8 to 12) reading with great accuracy of intonation, including music in two parts with dissonances of a semitone. In a letter to John Curwen he refers to the 'complete success of your system', going on to say, 'I was particularly interested by it, because during my researches in musical acoustics I came from theoretical reasons to the conviction that this was the natural way of learning music, but I did not know that it had been carried out in England with such beautiful results'. (Helmholtz, 1885, App. XVIII.)

A footnote mentions the Crystal Palace festivals of the tonic solfa-ists, where up to 5000 people took part in sight-reading, including an anthem by Macfarren (at that time a contemporary composer).

What could be done a century ago could be, and in some schools is still, done today. What is done depends upon priorities in both school and in teacher training. In my own, albeit limited, experience, the school where the general music education, in class, is based upon singing and vocal music reading, usually also produces good instrumental work. The instrumentalists have a better chance of being able to sing, at least 'inside them' (see p. 32) what they play.

Vocal music reading does not always imply sight singing, a term formerly used and now sometimes referred to with opprobrium. Often enough it is a matter of using the notation as a reminder of what is already known or partly known. Nevertheless, there are times when the singer needs to be able to realize in sound the notation of a piece of music that is entirely unfamiliar. When he can do this he has the means of exploring previously unknown music without external aid. This also applies to the instrumentalist; but vocal and instrumental music reading are not identical operations.

Wherein lies the important difference? Both have to perceive and understand the notation (the composer's instructions), and both express their understanding in physically produced sounds. However, it is the body itself, the voice, which produces the singer's sounds, and the voice requires no manipulation (in its more literal sense). Manipulation of an external agent, the instrument, causes the latter to emit sounds, not (we hope!) the human body itself. This is an important difference.

The *vocalist*, singing alone and unaccompanied, reads the visual symbols. In order to reproduce them vocally he must already have learnt what they mean in terms of relative pitch and duration. These he learns through listening, singing, listening (again) to his own vocal sounds, and associating those sounds with visual symbols. He experiences certain physical sensations particularly in the region of the larynx and other muscles associated with the act of phonation; but these sensations are extremely fine and difficult to locate or categorize. (I refer to the child and most adults; not to the highly trained singer.) No manipulation of an external agent is involved. He cannot use any other part of his body, for example hands or fingers (manipulation), to set his larynx to vibrate at, say, 440 Hertz in order to produce the note A. He can only 'think' (or imitate) the sound; such is the intimate association between brain and larynx that he then, having 'thought', has to do nothing more than phonate, and the sound of the required pitch emerges. But first he must know (have learnt) the intended sound(s).

The *instrumentalist* also reads the same visual symbols. For him, in order to produce on his instrument the composer's intended sounds, previous knowledge of those sounds is not essential, however desirable. The visual symbols instruct the instrumentalist to manipulate his instrument in a certain manner, which of course the instrumentalist has had to learn. This manipulation is a physical act, in itself requiring no musical, or tonal, thinking. The instrument is the agent which, if I may so express it, does the musical, the tonal, 'thinking'. Granted the instrumentalist may think a great deal about the music, about its logic, about the artistic deviations from the scientific mean that contribute to a satisfying performance, about phrasing, dynamics, and about the best way to use his body, and so to manipulate his instrument, to achieve these. This I would describe as peripheral musical thinking, if it is accepted that basic and essential musical thinking is tonal thinking: knowing the intended pitch of the notated sounds *before* the instrument produces them. Some instrumentalists acquire this ability to think tonally. Some, judging by their complete dependence on their instrument, which they may indeed manipulate relatively skilfully and artistically, do not.

The child uses his voice from birth, and through various stages acquires considerable skill in its use by the age of 3 to 4 years, not only in speaking but also by no means infrequently in singing little tunes that he has memorized. At every stage his vocal development and control appear to be in advance of manipulation, even that needed for clapping, tapping or playing percussion instruments rhythmically. This is quickly illustrated by asking a child or group of children to repeat in tapping or clapping the following, clapped or tapped fairly quickly

   (obviously no visual notation is
                                 used in this operation)

Then sing it on a monotone to the time names:

taa   taa   tafatefe   tate   taa   (or other syllables if preferred, but
                                        the time names are just as easy to
                                        remember and the most logical.)

and ask them to do likewise. (Note: 'sing' these *not* speak them). Unanimity in singing the response is normally much better than in the tapping or clapping, indicating finer control of the laryngeal and oral movements than of the grosser movements of the hands.

As the voice (larynx, tongue, lips) is under such fine, critical and easy control, it seems not unreasonable to treat it as the first and most important instrument in music education, including the operation of learning to read music. However as the singer must first think his sounds before he sings, he must learn the mental effects of intervals in pitch. This is facilitated by naming the two notes that comprise each pitch interval of a melody. The physical sensations accompanying this naming of constituent sounds can also assist in the learning process. What names are used is a matter of opinion: absolute pitch names (A B C D E F G) are favoured by some; relative pitch names (d r m f s l t—which are a form of shorthand for tonic, supertonic, mediant etc.) by others. The former *might* assist in developing that particular form of memory known as absolute pitch, especially if learnt at a very early age and that usually in association with an instrument (Sergeant, 1969, pp. 135–143); and of course the possessor of absolute pitch encounters few problems in reading even difficult modern music vocally. The relative pitch names—solfa—are probably still more widely used as the introduction to vocal music reading, and they have a long and respectable history of at least a thousand years. They can cope with all music, from the early modal to the highly chromatic, although they lose some of their efficacy with music that dispenses with tonality. Since most of the music that most people will sing, for a long time to come, is likely to have fairly recognizable tonality, it would seem unwise to discard this useful aid to vocal music reading before some other, more effective, means have been discovered.

One final word on this topic: Obviously, reading music is not an end in itself; it is only a means to the making of music. We can make some music without reading the visual symbols, but we can make a lot more when we can read them. The same idea applies to the reading of the English language. Furthermore, the symbols of music notation, both singly and in combination, are visually less complicated, and thus easier for the young child to grasp and interpret, especially vocally, than the convoluted squiggles of the letters of the English alphabet, again whether singly or in combination into words. The difference in practice is that we make a determined effort to teach language reading and give lots of practice; in music reading we do not.

Some modern ideas on music education

What do we mean by 'modern'? From some quarters we are being urged to be modern, forward-looking; sometimes, apparently, in different directions and towards very indistinct horizons. The music of the past is 'irrelevant' to the twentieth century child. The 'here and now' is all important.

> . . . music of our own day is more relevant to us and to our situation [upon which, it is maintained 'music makes a comment'] than music of any other time. To understand the art of the present is to understand ourselves. (Paynter & Aston, 1970, p. 201)

> . . . the music most relevant to our age is that which *differs* the most radically from previous music. (Dennis, 1972, p. 20)

> This book is written to help teachers who would like to introduce *truly modern music* to their classes. (Dennis, 1970, p. 1)

> Behold the new orchestra: the sonic universe. And the new musicians: anyone and anything that sounds. (Schafer, 1969, p. 2)

> The big sound sewer [sic] of the future will be the sky. (*ibid.*, p. 58.)

> The universe is your orchestra (*ibid.*, p. 62.)
> The new orchestra is the Universe (*ibid.*, p. 63.)

The above quotations are colourful and terse. I have selected them because they are currently widely read by teachers in schools; and the latter may be, and doubtless are, influenced by them, especially if they feel they must keep up with the times. But what do they mean?

It is well-known how musical composition, and apparently some non-composition, has changed in the last 70 years or so, and especially in the last 15 to 20 years: to the extent that some people now include as music any sound that we care to make. Some of it certainly 'differs . . . most radically from previous music'; in that sense I suppose it may be described as 'truly modern'. But what about the music of other equally contemporary composers, to quote only, for instance, that of Benjamin Britten, William Walton or Michael Tippett, whose reputations internationally as well as nationally are pretty high? It 'differs' from previous music as would every significant composer's latest work, but not 'most radically' in the sense of some really avant-garde experiments; yet is it not just as 'truly modern' and just as 'relevant to our age'? Is not this also 'music of our own day'? If indeed music can make a 'comment' on our 'situation' (whatever that means), do not Britten, Walton, Tippett and many other similar contemporary composers 'comment' as intelligibly as the more avant-garde experimenters? Furthermore, is it not conceivable that Bach, Mozart or Beethoven may help us to 'understand ourselves' as clearly as 'the art of the present'?

Let us recall that our concern is with education, mainly in school, and that the most important people are the children and their teachers. In order for it to be 'relevant' (blessed word in the 1970s) must their musical experience be confined to either the latest experiments of a few composers, or whatever the children can 'create' themselves in a superficially similar vein? Children and teachers being ordinary fallible human beings, this may not happen all the time, or even some of it, in most classrooms. But the implication is clear.

Again, keeping the reality of the school in mind, how do we bring Schafer's 'sonic universe' and especially that 'sewer', into the primary school classroom? And even if we could, how 'meaningful' (another contemporary blessed word) would it be?

Before accepting such statements as those quoted, we have a responsibility to demand what clearly observable, if not quantitively measurable, effects they have on the children.

At this point it might be of interest to consider the effects that some 'contemporary music' can have on adult professional musicians. The reporting is brief and thus probably does not tell the full story, but the reference is given (In: *Music and Musicians,* Feb. 1974, pp. 5–6) for the reader who cares to follow up the study:

Occupational Hazard
'Psychological problems found in wives of German orchestral players prompted two German psychologists, Marie-Luise Fuhrmeister

and Eckart Wiesenhutter, to do an in-depth survey of the musicians themselves. Their findings have been recently published under the title *Metamusik* in Munich.

They examined 208 players drawn from three different symphony orchestras. One of the orchestras played mainly classics, another's predominantly classical repertoire was liberally sprinkled with modern works and the third concentrated primarily on contemporary music. The players from the first orchestra were found to be mainly happy and well balanced people. However, those from the other two suffered in various ways, the players from the wholly contemporary orchestra being the worst affected.

More than 70 per cent of these players suffered from acute nervousness, and over 60 per cent from irritation and aggressive tendencies. More than 22 per cent became depressed or suffered from insomnia, headaches, earaches and diarrhoea. Smaller percentages complained of frequent abdominal pains, cardiac trouble and even impotence.

String players are the worst affected, followed by woodwind, and finally brass. In fact many string players find that they have lost their perfect pitch. Most of these players feel that their years of dedicated training are being wasted, and their true musical potential neglected. At home, where they practise their parts between rehearsals, their wives object to being subjected to unwelcome sounds.

Many of the players are demanding that they should be retired earlier than their predominantly classical colleagues. Perhaps the day is approaching when a modern composer will be cited in a divorce action?'

If this can happen to adults, is it not conceivable that concentration 'primarily on contemporary music' might have comparably disturbing effects on children?

It would seem that 'modern' ideas on music education tend to be concerned variously but mainly with

1. listening attentively to *any* sounds
2. being originally creative
3. providing experience of a new kind of 'music' to perform which requires very little effort and minimal skills
4. integration.

The first of these is one of Schafer's themes in his book *Ear Cleaning* (1967) and *The New Soundscape* (1969). The students should become more aware of the sounds of their environment, and of the sounds that they themselves can create from commonplace objects. (Conventional musical instruments, played in a conventional manner, have little part in this.) George Self (1967) and Brian Dennis (*op. cit.*) also give much attention to this aspect of listening. There is nothing fundamentally new in it; as long as forty years ago—and doubtless long before then— teachers were urging their pupils to use their 'powers of observation', aural as well as visual. What is 'new' or 'modern' in this is the idea that all these sounds may now be regarded as acceptable ingredients of music: 'anyone and anything that sounds'. But this can not be the whole story: The child's environment includes conventional music, and account must be taken of this. Observe the infant: He notices the difference between his own sound-creation (e.g. banging the tray of his high chair with a spoon) and his mother singing or conventional instrumental playing. The healthy baby already notices and reacts to many differences in sound: timbre, pitch, loudness.

Perhaps as we grow older we become so acclimatised to the noises that almost overwhelm daily life that we tend to ignore many of them, and listen (i.e. pay attention) only to those sounds that interest, or might interest, us. Just as in other multitudinous experiences of life, we grow more selective, so do we likewise in respect of the sounds that surround us. For this reason it is no bad thing to have our attention called to our sound environment from time to time. Listen: what can you hear? Much more than when you were not listening attentively. But are the sounds you hear 'music'?

To the sounds of the environment we can add the sounds we can make ourselves, with the body (clapping, stamping, mouth sounds that are different from 'singing') and those that can be made with other sound producing objects. We can hit or tap a chair leg and then the wooden seat: the resulting sounds will probably be of different pitch and timbre. We can even scrape a chair along the floor: that produces a sound that is not easy to describe. We can treat various metal objects in different ways and different sounds will emerge. We can even kneel on a wooden floor and move around an upturned glass ashtray: that too will produce sound. There are many ways of creating sound that, once our attention is focused upon them, are interesting. Doubtless they contain a germ of muscial potential: After all, the sounds of conventional musical instruments are generated by similar means: striking, scraping and blowing. But again the question must be asked: Are these other sounds that we have created 'music'?

It depends on how widely we define the term 'music'. If the 'fines' (the bounds implied in the word 'definition') are so wide as to include 'anyone and anything that sounds', then further attempts to define the term 'music' are useless. If Schafer is right, then we can call any sounds we hear, or make, 'music' and no one can deny us. Anything goes.

It may be argued that the kind of listening referred to above makes us more sensitive to sounds. Even that may be challenged. Normal hearing is sensitive enough to the sounds around us. What the foregoing is asking us to do is to pay conscious attention to that existing aural sensitivity: in other words to listen. Listening is an essential for music, but not just to everything within earshot; listening to music is selective listening.

Let us now consider the second concern of 'modern' ideas about music education: being originally creative. It is sometimes maintained that, given the sound producing instruments, and implements, the child will 'instinctively' create music, and that which he himself creates will have more meaning for him than that which he has not created. The latter part may contain an element of truth; but the instinct to create original music (whatever that is) does not appear to be universal (see pp. 41–43). Given the opportunity to play with sound producing instruments, many, perhaps most, infants will have a go for a short time. But then what happens? Some quickly become bored; others return from time to time, but by no means all find the sounds, and the bodily movements needed to produce them, of lasting interest.

Then again, the modern idea of creativity that is usually encouraged is musically unconventional. It must be 'new', and 'divergent' from the past. The kind of implements suggested make conventional music impossible, or where more conventional instruments are allowed they are to be used, or abused, in non-conventional ways. (Perhaps recent rocketing prices will discourage 'preparation' of pianos.)

This 'modern' creativity seems to be associated in the minds and writings of its promoters with the sounds of avant-garde experiments, something differing 'most radically from previous music'. When writing about George Self's 'simple notational shapes to represent not specific pitches and rhythms but types of sound and texture', Brian Dennis states:

This enabled the teacher to find an approximation in the classroom to many of the sounds of avant-garde music (Cage, Berio, Stockhausen, Penderecki and even Boulez). The system demonstrated how sophisticated as well as 'modern' a group of young musicians could sound particularly as each player added to the overall complexity of texture by playing different pitches, different rhythms, etc. In other words a large ensemble of youngsters was able to match in sound the virtuosity of a smaller number of professional players. (B. Dennis, *op. cit.*, p. 21)

Yet earlier Dennis had stated:

The extreme difficulty of Boulez and similar composers is that their music requires unprecedented technique of execution. (*Op. cit.*, p. 20)

One cannot have it both ways. If 'unprecedented technique of execution' is needed for the performance of certain pieces of music, how can we accept that relatively unskilled school pupils (however euphemistically described as 'young musicians') can 'match in sound' that which requires this 'unprecedented technique'. What have the 'professional players' been doing spending years of training and hard work acquiring their 'technique' if youngsters in school can 'match their virtuosity' without training or effort? And what, if they read the above quotation, would the composers Messrs Boulez & Co. think?

Again, on not dissimilar lines, Schafer writes concerning his own work:

A question often raised over the years at lectures and workshops has been: 'Where does it all lead?', and I suppose after ten years one ought to have an answer. But the easiest answer to give will be the hardest to take, and will not win many converts to creativity. 'Where does it all lead?' the Principal had asked after one of our more daring sessions, and looking desperately around the class at the debris, I fixed my eye on him firmly and said: 'Anarchy, anarchy' . . . . A totally creative society would be an anarchic society. (Schafeer, 1973, p. 4)

Perhaps teachers working in schools daily might relish the idea of Schafer's 'anarchy' for five days a week, twelve or more weeks a term; there are certainly many children, our main concern, who would not. In the interest of these children, even if not of their teachers, we are obliged to ask: Is this kind of activity educationally valid?

Let us now consider the third concern of some 'modern' ideas about music education: providing experience of a new kind of 'music' that requires very little effort and minimal skills. This seems to spring from some sort of missionary zeal for 'improving' musically incompetent (for whatever reason) teenagers. They must have some music of some sort. It is alleged that thus they will come to terms with their musical environment without, of course, any great effort. This, I suppose, could not be some form of 'do-good-ing'—not so different from the maligned efforts of many 19th century educators to bring a little light and joy into the lives of the working class? (They at least demanded some effort.)

Could one suspect a patronizing note in Schafer's statement:

> Different degrees of intelligence require different goals . . . . I am merely trying to point out that music education, geared down to the average human intelligence, may have its own rewards; and certainly it would be more appropriate for places like schools where average human beings congregate. (Schafer, 1973, p. 4)?

Or Dennis:

> It (i.e. the music of Boulez *et al.*) is music for a small intellectual elite and is likely to remain so however hard we try to swell the ranks. Whether we like it or not this is only the extreme manifestation of an elite-oriented tradition and very little of our so-called serious music can be exempt from this description. (*op. cit.*, p. 20)
>
> Few of them (i.e. the children in school) indeed are going to have a full appreciation of much of this 'exclusive' music . . . . Why not help create a new participatory music in which everyone can be involved and which can be enjoyed for itself and the activity it promotes? (*op. cit.*, p. 21)

Is there no fundamental appeal in music, social class and intelligence apart?

This attitude seems to suggest acknowledgement of the triangle or sieve 'theory' proposed earlier concerning developing attitudes and skills: The appeal of music will be considerable for some children and less for others; the development of skills of a more conventional musical kind will vary considerably, and by the time school pupils have reached the teen-ages a minority will have acquired considerable ability: the majority will not.

The concern is for the majority, and that concern is excellent if facilities and staffing are adequate to cope with all of them without neglecting the minority of musically able and willing. Usually in schools they are not adequate.

But there is a further implication concerning the unskilled majority:* If they cannot participate in conventional music, 'classical' or 'modern', we must find something they *can* do, with much participatory activity but minimal skills, with instant results preferably differing 'radically from previous music'; then call *that* 'music'.

Skills

'. . . technical skill and historical learning, etc. can never guarantee to develop musicality, i.e. the talent to create original music.'† (Cooper, 1974, p. 70)

This statement is true; it has already been discussed (pp. 00–00): The acquirement of skills cannot guarantee originality. But the converse, that we can create original music without some basic skills, is less convincing, unless we redefine, or rather un-define, the term 'music'. True originality, in music or any other form, is a rare occurrence even amongst those of exceptional 'skill and learning'. To pretend otherwise is to make nonsense of human endeavour.

The advocators of these 'modern' activities usually state that this is only a part of music education ('Creative experiment is only one small part of music education . . . .' (Paynter, p. 23)), and that the 'other' part of music education also has a place in the scheme of things ('The learning of traditional reading and playing techniques should be taught by practical means and I have no wish to supplant any of this valuable activity'. (Dennis, 1972, p. 21))

However, in practice, these 'creative' activities in school are by their nature so time-consuming that 'traditional reading and playing techniques' tend to be neglected. In any case, can we reasonably expect children to associate, let alone reconcile, the results of such creativity sessions, so radically differing from 'previous music', with 'traditional' music, and the effort required to achieve the skills necessary for playing it?

* I use the expression 'unskilled' in no denigratory sense; there is no disgrace in not wanting to play the violin or any other instrument.

† Many musicians, psychologists and others, from at the latest 1896 (Billroth, 1896), have been arguing about: what is musicality? Few would define the term so narrowly as 'the talent to create original music'.

Are there not other, equally valid if not so radically different, forms of creativity, based upon more traditional experience and skills? For example, the child who 'creates' his or her own four-phrase carol to be sung in a primary school: The format, the style, may be derivative, but it is truly original, and that child's own. Or the youngster who, after a few months' tuition on the piano, decides to create his own little piano piece within his limited technique: again derivative but, yet again, his own. Or the child who, having learnt a little solfa, makes up his or her own tune, and can sing it naming the constituent sounds: Is not this also creative and not 'irrelevant' to that child at that stage of experience? Such creative activities are, of course, based upon acquired skills.

Also in a modern idiom, albeit rather different from some of the proposals already discussed, Peter Maxwell Davies was encouraging some of his pupils at Cirencester Grammar School, some fifteen or so years ago, to compose music which was original and 'modern'. But whilst encouraging originality, he also states:

I taught them to read music and to sight sing music, and, in order to do this, one taught them traditional scales and notation, because *those are the things they find in use around them all the time* . . . in order for them to read traditional music, to play and sing it, we have to teach children basic techniques. (Schlotel, 1973, p. 14)

The present depends on the past, and this must not be ignored.

Elsewhere, Davies comments more generally about composition:

. . . any musical 'freedom' must know . . . from what it is supposed to be free, otherwise it can only be meaningless. We have, in 'advanced' musical circles, the sorry sight of the extreme products of this misinterpretation of freedom, who, misunderstanding what is involved, betray freedom, either by imposing order in the consequent limitless chaos of musical possibilities by reducing the composition process to the realization of predetermined formulae concerning pitch, note-length, dynamic, or, at the other extreme, of leaving the composition process to 'chance' elements, which process leads to complete musical meaninglessness, with the introduction of extra-musical stunts which are not even shocking, having no significance in any sense whatever. (P. Maxwell Davies, 1962, pp. 27–28.)

Integration

One popular 'modern' educational idea is that of 'integration'. Life is complex and not lived in separate compartments; life in school must reflect this, and therefore there must be no separate subject teaching. The various areas of learning must be integrated, and this must include music.

I have left this to the last of the four ideas, in order to concentrate earlier on music education itself. But the effect on music education of 'integrating' music with other non-musical activities must be considered briefly.

In the first place, music is essentially different from other experiences insofar as it is non-verbal. It is not dependent on words or numbers, or on ideas associated with these, as are other learning experiences, even including most crafts and art (excepting the purely non-representational). Music cannot be 'explained' except in its own non-verbal terms.

It can imitate or suggest external ideas, as in some programme music; it can create an impression. But the external ideas that a single piece of music suggests and the impressions it creates will vary enormously from listener to listener until the particular idea or impression has been spelled out in words; and even then the associations are tenuous.

Since music is so different from other experiences it needs to be treated differently from anything else. It exists in its own right as a separate human experience, and the skills involved in listening and more overt participation are to some extent unique. Integrate it with other learning situations and these musical skills tend to suffer.

This is by no means to deny the association of music with other activities. Obviously there are words, as in singing, and all that that implies; there are movement and dance with which it is closely associated, although these can exist without it. It can contribute to drama. There are many other possible and desirable associations of music with other activities. But association is not quite the same as integration.

In a recent survey of music education in the primary school (Reading University/Schools Council project, *op. cit.* 'Working Paper' 1973 not yet published, pp. 133/4), many music teachers, lecturers and advisers expressed concern "that continual 'integration' (of music) with other aspects of the curriculum was incompatible with the systematic development of musical skills . . . there was no opposition to the principle of 'integration' provided that this did not preclude the separate pursuit of music for itself . . . . From our observation of the use of music in 'integrated' work, we formed the impression that music often fared badly in such circumstances. . . . A distinction is now frequently made between 'integrated' and 'related' studies. In the former a 'topic' may be chosen and treated in a number of ways, one of which might involve the use of music. In the latter a relationship between two (or more) particular subject areas is explored. As music educators we see more potential value in the relating of music to other areas (for which there is so much scope), than in the extremely chancy or cursory treatment it might suffer in the 'topic' approach, when, all too frequently, some song or record is incorporated into the 'project' 'because it happens to fit the subject', with little musical significance or benefit."

These are opinions not to be lightly ignored.

Listening to contemporary music

The discussion so far in this chapter has been concerned with active participation by the children, apart from the paragraphs on listening to ambient sounds. No mention has been made of just listening to contemporary, including avant garde, music. It has to be accepted that most teachers and young instrumentalists do not have the technique to play most of it, so we have to resort to recordings, which, although a second best to live performance, will give a truer representation of the composer's intentions than some of the classroom 'approximations' mentioned earlier.

Just as it is important for the children to hear music from earlier days which they cannot themselves perform, so they should be given opportunity to hear music of their own day. The important point to bear in mind is that there are many styles and periods of music, and it is our duty to acquaint our pupils with the most outstanding of these.

The results of electronic composition would not be excluded from such listening.* From electronic devices, as yet barely 20 years old we are already getting exciting new sounds in both 'serious' and 'pop' music. Future developments will doubtless add more. How far they will

* It is appreciated that a few schools now possess synthesizers and other means of electronic composition, but so far only a very tiny proportion of pupils can have access to these. Furthermore, electronic composition demands specialized knowledge and skills other than those normally associated with music, and can take an inordinately long time. Live performance, in any way comparable to conventional performance, and apart from the playing of tapes, is as yet impossible on any but the most sophisticated and expensive apparatus.

be incorporated into, and settle down in, the mainstream of music remains to be seen.

Fashions and a plea for balance

Never chase a bus, a man (woman) or an educational idea: There is another coming along soon.

A major function of education is to enable our children to come to terms with their present, and to prepare them, as far as we can foresee, for the future. Thus we need the constant challenge of new ideas; but 'new' does not necessarily mean better. We come to terms with our present through the inevitable conditioning of at least the immediate past. As to the future, it would be arrogant of anyone to pretend to *know* what it holds for us, either in general terms or in music. The most we can do is to seek present trends, where they are discernible, and guess about the future.

Whilst welcoming new ideas, it is also our duty to challenge them. Before accepting them we need to be assured by how much and in what way they are better than existing ideas. Too carefree an adoption of the latest, which may not have been put to the test and proved superior, can affect a whole generation of children.

Fashions in music change, fashions in education change; fashions in music education also change. Each generation of human beings tries to effect change if only to assert its own identity. Adolescents need parents as something to rebel against, however mildly. These growth-through-adolescence pains are a recurring feature; they should not take us, parents and/or teachers, by surprise. We must be prepared to cope with them through a combination of flexibility of ideas and firmness. Flexibility of ideas is essential in order to maintain communication with the young; firmness, adherence to principles and standards, are equally important if society is not to be embroiled in utter chaos every twenty-five years.

In any case, does the human animal change so fundamentally, so radically with every generation? In contrast with some violent changes in environment that have occurred in the twentieth century (the externals of living), the genetic evolution of man is an infinitely slower process.

It is not realistic to expect a 'deep change in human nature' to occur suddenly because science and technology in a few years increases the power of destruction a thousandfold. Does the rate of mental and social evolution of the human race have to be adapted to the rate of change of his technological environment or should the rate of change of the latter be slowed down to what is acceptable to the former? (Maddock, 1972, p. 343)

This statement and question might well be applied to music and music education.

Do we, as educators anxious to be up-to-date with the most recently propounded ideas, sometimes overlook this slower, more fundamental adaptation to changing externals? In asking this question I have in mind, in particular, the earlier years of life up to, shall we say, the age of about thirteen years before most children begin, noticeably, to rebel; and I am also thinking of music education as a part of general education.

The child of the 1970s matures, in the fundamental, as distinct from the superficial, sense, in a manner very similar to the child of the 1950s or 1940s; perhaps even to the child of one hundred or more years ago. He doubtless has greater opportunity for accelerated development of his innate proclivities; and we hope that he will be the better person for this; although we may not yet have proved this in the long term.

What has happened to music in many schools for young children? Fashions have changed. In most schools music is a minority time subject, and within the limited time available only a certain amount can be achieved; the introduction of new activities tends to oust former activities.

'Whenever you add anything fresh to the curriculum you must inevitably take something out, and state honestly what it is, and why?' (Lord James, 1972.)

The record player, and inexpensive instruments, became available in the 1920s and 1930s. We had the 'appreciation' movement: sit and listen to gramophone records—relatively easy for the teacher! We had non-pitch percussion bands. We had the recorder. We had pitch percussion instruments. Now we have electronic devices that can create sounds that are quite different from anything that was conceivable twenty years ago.

This is certainly change. It is equally certainly progress, in the sense of forward, or onward, movement; but is the movement always in the right direction? I do not know the answer, but I suggest that periodically we ought to stop and think. Increased technology can be a great boon, but it tends to become increasingly depersonalized.

Yet participation in music involves bodily activity and that is a highly personal response. Instruments apart, the body can produce a variety of sounds, percussive by movement of the limbs, and tonal (including pitch, duration, timbre, dynamics) via the voice. Before adopting some new 'progressive' fashions that neglect the voice, we should pause and ask ourselves if we are in fact 'progressing' in the right direction.

In pausing to take stock of our ideas, ideals and aims about the music education of the young, we should not neglect the body itself, and particularly the voice, as a musical instrument, intimate and under the most sensitive control of the child, and thus the easiest of all instruments to 'play'.

My emphasis on the most intimate, and easiest, form of music making must not be interpreted as denigration of the enormous growth of instrumental playing in the last twenty-five years; I only plead for a balance.

We also need to pause and think critically when we hear disparaging remarks about the past, remembering that music existed in all classes (working, middle, or other) before the second half of the 20th century.

I once heard a 'modern' composer refer to Victorian hymn tunes as 'musical obscenities'. This sounded rather splendid until one thought about it: What is a 'musical obscenity'? And even if someone will define it in 1975, will the definition hold in 1995, or will that particular composer's works by then have been similarly classified? The Victorians at least enjoyed singing and playing their hymn tunes, as indeed do many of our contemporaries, witness the teen-age schoolgirl who recently had this to say: 'When we sing a good hymn in school assembly it sends shivers up your spine'. She was referring to a late nineteenth century hymn tune. Obscene? Who or what was obscene? The music? The girl? The sensation she experienced?

It is easy to be clever at the expense of someone else. At the present time it is fashionable to denigrate the past. When a composer does this, in categorical and colourful statements, there are always some less eminent, including some music educators, who will be influenced and unthinkingly quote him, in their desire to be thought modern.

As educators is our prime concern with fashion? It might appear so; so numerous are the new nostrums being offered. But must we un-thinkingly accept these? It is suggested by some that children would more readily accept, and be able to perform, not only instrumentally, but also vocally, a-tonal idioms if they were made to listen to more of such music in school, and were deprived of early experience of tonal composition. But is this a practical proposition, apart from the Platonic idea of removing the baby from its parents? And are we sure that such is the music of the future? Is there no musical tradition that we ought to hand on? One further question: How much of such new music can young children play, let alone sing, for themselves?

These are some matters of concern for teachers and those who train them. We are witnessing rapid and fascinating technological changes, and the human organism may gradually, and slowly, adapt to these; but it can only do it, as it were, via its own intimate body and brain. It is particularly important to remember this in regard to music, where the initial response is primarily emotive and physical; and where the younger the child, the more intimate the response.

If music is to be an integral part of a child's general schooling, then his teacher must be aware of his needs and his abilities. Abilities may vary between children of any given age, but whatever the pupil's current abilities, his developmental needs are not dissimilar. They start from the use of the body in singing and in increasing co-ordination of limb movements. He first makes music with his own body. We can then extend this to other, external, instruments that require manipulation, with no bodily created sound; but we continue to use the body as a musical sound-producing instrument in itself and not solely as a silent manipulator. This latter use of the body, solely as a manipulator, has been, unfortunately, happening in many of our schools during the last quarter century.

Fashions in music and in education change almost as quickly as fashions in women's clothes, but, fortunately, fashions in women's clothes do not significantly affect the female body; they are merely external (and expensive!) superficial trappings. Much more importantly fashions in education can affect whole generations of children.

It is our duty to be aware of, and to make our future teachers aware of, current ideas in both new musical composition and in educational theory. But it is equally important to hand on from one generation to the next our heritage of what is good in both material and method, together with the highest standards of excellence that we can possibly attain.

Chapter Four

Evaluation

'How am I doing?' The interested pupil wants to know. He may not ask the question outright in so many words, but it may be seen in his inquiring glance; and he wants an answer.

I speak of the 'interested' pupil. Obviously the pupil who is not interested would not ask the question. Equally obviously the arousal and maintenance of interest is a function of the teacher. Furthermore, interest is inevitably linked with aims, objectives or goals. These may be long-term in the mind of the teacher, but for the pupil they must also, and primarily, be short-term, something realistically attainable within, say, a week, or a lesson, within minutes, or even immediately. These goals, short- or long-term, must be clearly defined, and intelligible to the pupil. He must know what exactly he is expected to do; otherwise how can he do it?

Let us take a simple example of an extremely short-term aim:

The teacher sings   G E G E   A G E—
        or   s m s m   l s m—

and asks the pupil to sing it back. He does so, correctly; he has achieved the defined goal. Another, who sings it incorrectly, has not; he needs more help and another try.

Another short-term aim:

The teacher shows the pupil how to play the same seven-note (actually only three different notes) tune on the recorder. The pupil plays it back correctly and the aim is achieved; incorrectly and the aim is not achieved, so he is given more help and makes more effort (another try).

A longer-term aim is exemplified by the instrumental teacher who specifies, realistically we hope, how much of a sonata movement should be prepared for the next lesson a week hence.

And of course for some pupils the much longer term aim is a concert performance in, say, six weeks' time, or an examination in a year's time; such performances or examinations are occasions on which one can demonstrate what one has been doing in the meantime by way of preparation.

Broadly speaking, the younger the child the shorter-term the objective needs to be; but long- or short-term, the objective must be clearly stated. Otherwise, how can he know what to aim for? If the objective is not clearly stated, the question might be not 'how am I doing?' but 'am I on the right road?' or even 'on the map?'

Could it be that some class music teaching is not even 'on the map'? One sometimes wonders where it is supposed 'to be going'.

In class work, objectives must be realistic, and so pitched that they will be attainable by the majority of pupils. 'Success breeds success' applies here as elsewhere. Although not all may succeed equally well, the teacher who sets objectives that are not realistically attainable by the majority of a class is out of touch with the individuals in that class, and, if the objectives are not immediately revised, will fail; and it is the teacher who is failing, not the pupils.

We set objectives for class work with the intention that the majority in the class will achieve them; we do not aim at failure. Nevertheless, there will be some children, hopefully a minority, who do fail to achieve the objectives, and it is no use the teacher pretending that those children have not failed to achieve the goal. The teacher knows; what is much more important, the children themselves know. Whether we like it or not, they compare themselves and their achievements, or lack of them, with their fellows and what they can do. To say 'That's good' when the child knows it is not good serves no useful purpose at all. The only outcome from such a situation is the child's loss of esteem for the integrity of the teacher.

This does not imply that the teacher should not continue to give the child every possible help and encouragement, ultimately perhaps by setting more easily attainable objectives, and by praising those which he does achieve; but dishonest praise for non-achievement is a waste of time, especially for the pupil.

Evaluation is more than measurement, tests or examinations but, formal or informal, these are an integral part of it. The answer to 'Can

I do it?' can only be given as a result of some form of testing. The not uncommon current idea that tests and examinations are degrading and undignified is not only emotionally charged but, in terms of even sheer existence, unrealistic. Evaluation is integral in living and learning.

> . . . man adapts to and overcomes his environment by constantly saying to himself 'How am I doing?' then 'How can I do better?' The second question is essential for progress, but it is always preceded by the first question, and that is evaluation. (Colwell, 1970, p. 1)

We set ourselves goals. We try to reach them. If we reach them, the goals we had set were realistically attainable; and on the way we learnt something about how we reached them, in other words, the methods; something perhaps to be repeated because the methods were successful. If we do not reach the goals, either they were not realistically attainable, or the methods we used were inappropriate, or perhaps we had been lazy, or were just not able. All the time we are testing ourselves. The only part of this operation that could be called degrading or undignified is when we have set ourselves, or been set, a realistically attainable goal and then been too lazy to try to reach it. Furthermore, there is no degradation or indignity in not being able to do everything that some-one else may be able to do.

The private studio teacher and the peripatetic teacher of individuals or small groups in schools are evaluating at every lesson: their pupil's progress, or reasons for lack of it; their own teaching techniques, which include interpersonal relationships between teacher and pupil; the goals they set, and whether or not their pupils achieve them.

Compared with the classroom teacher of thirty or more pupils, the violin teacher, for example, has a relatively simple (not necessarily easy) task: in a small group of, say, 5 or 6 children, to teach Willie to play the violin sensitively and with some musical understanding. In trying to teach Willie to play the violin, that teacher sets many short-term objectives from lesson to lesson: e.g. to play open strings, then with one finger, then two, and so on. He, or she, can say when Willie has reached a reasonably definable stage. Grade examinations help the teacher to define progress. In spite of some criticisms levelled against them, such examinations can also act as an incentive and a further source of motivation to the interested pupil; the objectives are clearly stated.

Furthermore these peripatetic teachers have been chosen because of their acknowledged competence in that particular field; and they are dealing with only a small, usually willing, minority of the school population, by whatever means the pupils may have been selected.

So far we have been mainly and properly concerned with the pupil and how he is doing. He will continue to be our chief centre of interest. Education is for him; but the teacher plays the key role: He is the servant, the principal medium through which the child becomes educated; or the one who provides the media through which the child educates himself. Without the stimulus, motivation, explanation of the teacher, providing the 'mind to mind' contact, most of the other media (sometimes grandly referred to as 'educational technology') are of little avail.

Therefore, the servant in this key position, the teacher, must be constantly evaluating himself: his aims, his various methods of achieving these, and the materials he provides. It is axiomatic to say that he must also 'understand' his pupils, but such 'understanding' is not a pheno-menon that exists in isolation from his aims, methods and materials. There is a reciprocal interaction between aims, methods and materials on the one hand, and 'understanding' on the other. The more the teacher examines, and where necessary revises, the former in the light of the results they achieve, the greater will be the latter: his 'under-standing'. In the examination, and possible revision, of aims, methods and materials, with an eye on objectives, he is testing himself and his own teaching; and such testing inescapably involves testing his pupils.

The testing may be informal or formal; the pupils may not always be aware that they are being tested; but the teacher, if there is such, who maintains that he *never* tests or examines his pupils, from the infant school upwards, is either dishonest or positively dangerous from the point of view of his pupils' development.

'If a teacher is too busy to give standardized tests, or to construct good tests of his own, he needs to re-examine the nature of his objectives and activities to see what is really being accomplished in his music program.' (Colwell, *op. cit.*, p. 47)

This applies to music education as well as to any other aspect of teaching and learning.

'Untested teaching is disappointing to all—to the teacher as well as to the pupil. . . . We never know that we have taught a pupil anything till we have got it back again from that pupil.' (John Curwen, 1875, p. 155)

Almost a century later (1970) we find Colwell making a comparable statement: 'A major value of testing and measuring is in the feedback. Both teacher and student can continually assess progress.' (Colwell, *op. cit.*, p. 26)

Tests however informal or formal, are the means by which the teacher can increase his knowledge and understanding of his pupils, and of the efficacy, or otherwise, of his teaching. Their object is not primarily to find fault; but if they do reveal weaknesses such revelation can provide clues for remedy; without such revelation the weaknesses may become chronic, to the lasting deprivation of the child.

I have written at some length about testing. The testing is the means of discovering if goals, immediate or long-term, are being achieved. This may be an appropriate moment to ask the question: testing for what? Which raises the thorny question of the overall purpose, or purposes, of music education in school.

The general welfare of the pupil, and his satisfaction in personal development from childhood onwards, is the overall objective of schooling. Every good teacher, of every subject or area of learning, is concerned with this. The music teacher shares this general concern with other colleagues. But he must also have objectives more specifically related to his own subject: music. Of him we may ask: Why teach music in school?

Such aims as immediate enjoyment, providing the means of leisure time activities for the golden age when the working man will have increased spare time, aesthetic appreciation—these, and many other comparable aims, can be achieved otherwise than through music: for example, through games, literature and drama, crafts and fine arts.

Music can only be justified as a school activity, like any other school activity, on the grounds that it provides a unique experience, however much it may be associated with other learning experiences during school life.

Thus the objectives of music education must also be unique, and concerned with music itself; always, of course, since we are dealing with education, in relation to the child. The answer I propose to the question: Why teach music in school? is: In order that the pupil may become acquainted with music (in at least some of its many forms and styles), thus come to know some music, learn to understand something of its essential features, *possibly* to 'appreciate' it. He will do this through listening to music and through active participation of bodily movement, singing, playing instruments, always at the appropriate level for his stage of maturation and development.

It is *music* education that we are dealing with, and objectives must be stated in terms of music. If these objectives cannot be justified as valid for activities in school, then music *qua* music has no place in the school curriculum.

Objectives should keep in mind what are generally considered to be important factors in a well-balanced curriculum, based upon the content of music itself; not upon the whim of the moment, nor on what is merely easy or just fun to do, nor even on what has been done in the past merely because it has been done.*

Children and teachers are not the only ones concerned with evaluation in education generally and in music education in particular. There are also the parents, who are concerned about their children's development, and who pay ever increasing rates and taxes towards the cost of the public sector of education, and, additionally, in the case of the private sector, ever increasing school fees. There are also the educational administrators; and the politicians, national and local, who raise taxes and rates and distribute the money for education. They too, quite reasonably, may ask—in my view, ought to ask continually—the sort of questions that challenge us, as educators, to justify what we are doing in the name of education, including music education. Are we making optimum use of our pupils' time? Indeed, are we making the best use of the vast sums of money devoted to schooling?

Teachers and others intimately involved in education might find such questions irksome, but that is no reason why they should not be asked, and even less reason why educators should not attempt to give more convincing answers than 'teacher knows best'. The questioners are asking for effective evaluation: for a statement of objectives, of the methods we use, and the effectiveness of these methods in achieving the objectives.

---

* There seems little danger of mere reliance on the past happening at present; some music educators appear all too anxious to jettison not only past methods but past music. (See pp. 53-60 above) The greater danger is that, in their efforts to be contemporary and up-to-date, with the third millenium AD in mind, they will also jettison that of the past that still remains truly worthwhile.

We may answer that music is a pervading phenomenon in our lives, and that therefore children should be given the opportunity to come to terms with it, to understand it, to appreciate it; furthermore, that it is a unique phenomenon, different from any other of life's experiences, and thus should not be neglected in schooling, however useless it may be in terms of vocation or profession.

Such an answer may be fair enough, but does it go far enough? The questioner may accept it but, reasonably, probe a little farther: As a result of what happens to him in school what more does the pupil know of music, or about music? Or, what can he do? Can he sing something, and how well? Can he play some instrument, and what can he play? Let us hear it. Can he read the notation of music and so explore it for himself? What does he know of the various forms and styles of music? What does he know of the people who compose it, who perform it? Can the pupil compose music?

Such questions are more practical than the more speculative and philosophical concerning 'appreciation', 'understanding', what 'good' it does to the pupil, or how 'much better' he is for it. These latter questions, and the like, cannot be answered with any degree of precision; we do not *know*, we can only speculate. But the more practical questions can be answered specifically, because they refer to specific behaviours. They may be less esoteric than the 'philosophical' questions, but they are not necessarily the worse for that.

There are some teachers who dislike such specific questions about knowledge of, and practical achievement in, music. They are inclined to think solely, or mainly, about the affective aspects: Music is to be enjoyed by all, musical skills and knowledge are irrelevant. If a class comes to, or starts, a music lesson looking forward to it, then in a vague way that is one aspect of evaluation: They obviously like music, or the teacher as a person, or both. This happens sometimes, but by no means always, even with the same group of children. The answer to the question: 'Why teach music to these children?' may be: 'because they like it'. Rather vague. The answer to a further question: '*Why* do they like it?' may be a little less vague, but is still elusive. There may be many diverse reasons; for example, 'because Mr X is amusing' or 'he doesn't notice what we are doing' (so we get on quietly with our homework!) or 'because he works us hard and makes it interesting', (these two, hard work and interest, often go together; most healthy children will respond to a realistic challenge to achieve something).

Of course we hope that children will enjoy their music, and other, lessons; but we have no means of measuring how much they enjoy them, either as a group or individually. By asking them, individually, *why* they enjoy, or do not enjoy, music lessons we can learn something rather more specific, and that specificity is often found to be associated with achievement, or lack of it: 'because I can do (or cannot do) what Mr X wants us to do'. (In addition to 'do' we might also use the words 'and know'.) Back we come again to well-defined objectives and methods of achieving them.

A mainly or solely affective, 'appeal-to-the-emotions', 'development-of-feeling' approach to music cannot be sustained. Knowledge and skills are enlisted from the earliest stages. The teacher provides the means of experience, which in the case of music always involves listening, whether or not the children are taking an active part through singing, playing or other movement. As they listen to the 'tune' they come to know it. When they know it they react to it, favourably or otherwise: like or dislike. They cannot react to something they do not 'know'. The source of such knowledge may be almost irrelevant: It may be a melody created by a child, vocally or instrumentally, or by the teacher, by Mozart, Brahms or Britten, performed live by a child or the teacher or via the record player, radio or television. As it is listened to, it becomes one bit more of musical knowledge to which the child may react, favourably or unfavourably.

The presentation of the 'tune' by the teacher may indeed be suggestive: 'Listen to this lovely "tune" (or "music")'. If the children approve of the teacher at that moment, the majority may succumb to the suggestion 'lovely', but we can never be sure. As visual beauty is 'in the eye of the beholder' so, comparably, aural (musical) beauty is 'in the ear of the listener'. Even if they approve of the teacher, there may be some children who still do not regard the 'tune' (music) as 'lovely'.

This is by no means to decry the idea that 'enthusiasm is catching'. Of course the enthusiastic teacher is likely to stimulate greater interest for the sources of his enthusiasms than the teacher who has none. This is a common experience not only in music and the arts but also in other less artistic areas of learning; and an experience to be encouraged.

But it has to be accepted that enthusiasms are not always caught, especially initially, however disappointing that may be to the enthusiastic teacher; and it must also be accepted that enthusiasm may develop, more slowly but sometimes more lastingly, through increasing knowledge and skills. These latter, knowledge and skills, can be taught by the teacher, and, according to their individually varying abilities, learnt by the pupils.

In order for knowledge and skills to be acquired (learnt) by the pupils, they must be aware of *what* they are expected to learn (objectives) and given indications as to *how* they may optimally, that is most easily and effectively, achieve them (methods).

Thus the teacher's main function is to impart knowledge and skills as appropriate; or phrased another way: to provide experiences through which the pupil may acquire knowledge and skills. How he does this depends to some extent on personality and enthusiasms; but however enthusiastic he may be, and accepting that his enthusiasm may be caught by at least some of his pupils, all he can teach is knowledge and skills.*

The teacher who accepts that, whatever his ultimate aspirations, his immediate function is to enable his pupils to acquire knowledge and skills, is in a stronger position to establish realistic objectives and to devise methods of achieving them, which he can put to the test to ascertain if they are in fact realistic and effective. This way lies progress for his pupils, and increased knowledge to which they can react and about which they will develop attitudes. He cannot be sure that his pupils will adopt the attitudes he hopes for, but, accepting that attitudes are based upon knowledge, he has at least given them a chance.

The opinion is sometimes expressed that tests ignore the 'feeling' aspect of music, and spoil the pleasure that could otherwise be derived from it. Certain it is that they require concentration, and some effort. What, that is worthwhile, in education does not?

However the experience of music educators *who do use tests from time to time* does not lend credence to the above opinion. There is much evidence to indicate that many† children enjoy periodic tests: as something to work towards, and as a challenge in the doing of them; and both these features can assist in the learning process. It all depends upon what exactly is meant by the 'feeling' aspect of music and 'pleasure'.

---

* If the teacher is uninterested and uninteresting he can still try to teach knowledge and skills; but if his approach is so dull as to fail to arouse interest on the part of his pupils he may be doing more harm than good (not making optimum use of his pupils' time—see p.73); in that case his pupils would be better employed using the time in some other area of learning.

† I avoid the word 'all' because we can never know enough about the human organism to be so dogmatic.

Standardized tests of achievement

So far I have been concerned mainly with tests devised by a teacher in relation to his own pupils, the work he has done with them and the means of assessing whether or not his objectives are being, or have been, achieved, whether within five minutes or five months.

This situation is restricted to one particular teacher and those pupils only for whom he is responsible. Many teachers are not satisfied with such a blinkered situation. They want to know how what they are doing, and their pupils' achievements, compare with the activities of teachers and the achievement of pupils, of comparable age, in different schools, localities and even countries. Most teachers are not satisfied to stay in their own little corner and ignore the world outside.

In these circumstances, standardized achievement tests have value for the purpose of comparison. As a result of using such standardized tests Mr X may discover that a large number of children, of the same ages as his own pupils, can achieve more than he and his pupils are doing. He asks: If they can do this, why cannot we? He begins a self-examination of objectives and methods; perhaps both were inadequate. Such critical and positive self-examination can lead to improvement in his own teaching.

Hopefully, he does not fall back on excuses such as 'my children could not do that', or blame entirely the socioeconomic environment of his pupils. Admittedly a poor environment can make life harder for him and his pupils, but that is no excuse for not making a strenuous effort to counteract and overcome the environmental influence. In any case, there is often a vast difference in the performance and achievements of pupils in different schools but from the same, or very similar, environments, good or not so good. Schooling that makes no difference (see p. 20) is not education.

The word 'standardized' indicates that a test, or battery of tests, has been tried out on very large numbers of children in many localities nationally and possibly internationally. The scores are set out in a way that enables teachers to see what the subject (i.e. the children tested) can do: usually indicating at least the mean, or average, score and the range of scores (highest to lowest individual scores) for each year age group. Other more technical details may also be given.

Even the non-statistically minded teacher can understand the simpler data of mean score and score ranges. He may discover that, say, 5,000 children aged 9 years have a mean score of 54 per cent correct within a range of 93 per cent to 11 per cent in a particular test. If his own 9 year old pupils score a mean of 62 per cent within a range of 87 per cent to 15 per cent in the same test, he may feel a degree of satisfaction that he is not doing too badly in comparison with many children, and their teachers, elsewhere. There is no need to moralize about an opposite result.

Only a few achievement tests have been standardized and published in English. All of these are American, and thus related to the American scene of music education. However, British teachers can learn much from them; there might be small superficial differences in philosophy and approach (much smaller differences than exist between some individual music educators in England), but the fundamentals of music are the same.

The reader who wishes to learn more about these published achievement tests is referred to Chapter Eight of *Evaluation of Music Teaching and Learning*. (Colwell, 1970). Only four of the published tests listed are applicable to general music education in school; these are the tests devised by W. A. Knuth, R. Colwell himself, A. Snyder Knuth, and Kwalwasser and Ruch. The Aliferis and Aliferis—Stecklein tests mentioned are aimed at college level, but could be useful also in secondary school work. The Watkins—Farnum Performance Scales, for wind and stringed instruments are, as the title implies, devised only for instrumental performance, from very elementary to more advanced levels.

A very brief description of the aims and contents of the first four mentioned above will give some indication of these attempts to measure achievement. All were based upon common practice and text books used in American schools.

1. *Achievement Tests in Music,* 'Recognition of Rhythm and Melody'. William A. Knuth 1936. Revised but not changed 1967.
   'The student hears a performance of complete musical phrases and is directed to find the error between the notation and the music he has heard.' (Colwell, *op. cit.*, p. 144)

2. *Music Achievement Tests,* Richard Colwell, 1970.
   'Four separate tests, each containing three or four sub-tests . . . Test 1 covers the area of pitch discrimination, interval discrimination, and meter discrimination. Test 2 includes auditory-visual discrimination. Test 3 consists of tonal memory, melody recognition, and instrument recognition. Test 4 has sub-tests on

style, texture (monophonic, polyphonic, homophonic), auditory-visual rhythm, and chord recognition.' (Colwell, *op. cit.*, p. 148)

3. *Snyder Knuth Music Achievement Test,* Alice Snyder Knuth, 1968.
'. . . designed to measure an individual's ability to understand musical notation . . . composed of four parts . . . listening and seeing . . . listening . . . musical comprehension . . . tonal memory . . . The basic elements of music, rhythm, melody, and harmony are not separated but appear as they normally do in music. Folksong material used by children in the public schools is the main source of test item material.' (Colwell, *op. cit.*, pp. 150–151)

4. *Kwalwasser—Ruch Test of Musical Accomplishment for Grades Four through Twelve* (i.e. 10—18 years), Jacob Kwalwasser and G. M. Ruch . . . Revised edition 1927, last printed 1952.
'The authors state that . . . the items . . . represent materials that public school students reasonably can be expected to master in the course of the first twelve grades . . . (6 to 18 years). There are ten sub-tests: (1) knowledge of musical symbols and terms; (2) recognition of syllable (i.e. solfa) names; (3) detection of pitch errors in a familiar melody; (4) detection of time errors in a familiar melody; (5) recognition of pitch names; (6) knowledge of time signatures; (7) knowledge of key signatures; (8) knowledge of note values; (9) knowledge of rest values; and (10) recognition of familiar melodies from notation.' (Colwell, *op. cit.*, p. 153)

It will be noted that these four published achievement tests are concerned with the materials of music. Some would say 'theory'; but if 'theory' it is, it is not theory divorced from practice. Three, those by Knuth, Snyder Knuth, and Kwalwasser and Ruch, are essentially concerned with notation and the sounds it represents, and parts of Colwell's tests also involve the use of notation linked with sounds: the auditory-visual discrimination, melody and chord recognition.

None of these tests claims to measure, or assist in the evaluation of, the whole of the music curriculum or musical development of the child. No test constructors would be so foolish. What they do measure are certain aspects of achievement that form a useful general background of the knowledge of the 'stuff' of music and skill in the use of it. These are aspects that can be measured objectively, and by means of group tests. Certain other aspects are amenable only to subjective measurement of individuals, for example instrumental and vocal performance, and composition.

Before leaving the subject of evaluation and achievement testing, mention should be made of two recent achievement tests for group application that were devised by Dr R. M. Thackray (1974, pp. 1–19 and 121–125) as part of a University of Reading/Schools Council project on the 'Music Education of Young Children'. They cannot be described as 'standardized' because the number of children who worked them is too small; for the first test 329 boys and girls aged 10 to 11 years in ten schools in one part of England; the second test has not yet been extensively applied. Furthermore, they were devised, not upon work which it was known had actually been done with all the children involved, but, with the collaboration of the ten teachers taking part in the experiment, as representing a 'realistic standard of musical achievement for children (in the last year of the primary school stage) who had received a reasonably sound foundation of teaching'. In each test the children had to respond, in writing on prepared answer forms, to musical material presented on tape. A brief description of the content of the tests follows.

Musical Achievement Test I*

'The twelve questions fell into three groups: the first four involved some aspect of pitch perception. Questions 5 to 8 were concerned with some aspect of rhythm (tempo, metre, duration of sounds, phrasing). The last four involved the linking of sound with some form of symbol. All instructions were given in full on the tape recording provided.

In more detail the questions were as follows:

Pitch (1—4)

1. Short tunes were played on chime bars and children had to say how many different chime bars (i.e. different pitches) were used in each.

2. Tunes of six notes were played and children had to mark which note was either the highest or the lowest.

3. Tunes were played consisting of either *small steps*, or *large leaps* or *a mixture* of the two. Children had to decide which of these three kinds of pitch movement applied.

---

* The tests were referred to as 'Quizzes'.

4. Two pairs of notes were played and children had to say which pair was *farther apart*.

Rhythm (5—8)

5. Children had to decide which of the following applied to the tunes they heard:
   A) gets quicker
   B) gets slower
   C) gets quicker, then slower
   D) gets slower, then quicker
   E) stays the same tempo throughout.
6. Children had to say which of the following applied:
   A) the music stays in 2 time all the way through
   B) the music stays in 3 time all the way through
   C) starts in 2 time and changes to 3
   D) starts in 3 time and changes to 2
7. Children had to mark the longest note in 7 note tunes.
8. Children had to decide which of the following applied to the two phrase tunes that were played:
   A) both phrases the same length
   B) longer phrase followed by shorter
   C) shorter phrase followed by longer

Sounds and Symbols (9—12)

9. Children were asked to match the tunes they heard with a graphic representation of them on the answer sheet.
10. Tunes with repeated rhythmic patterns were played. Children had to identify the pattern from the rhythmic notation given.
11. Tunes were played and children had to match them with the notation given (pitch and rhythm).
12. Children had to show where a tune was stopped in the middle by marking the place in the notation.

Results (brief summary only)

There were five items in each question, making a possible total of 60. In view of the variety of schools and teaching, a fairly wide range of marks was expected, but it was thought that mean scores would probably fall mainly within the 30—40 range. This for the most part proved to be the case, as the following table of results shows:

Table 1: Mean scores and ranges for full battery for ten classes of top juniors (ages 10—11 years).

School	N	Mean Score (Max. 60)	Range
B	40	38·8	53—24
H	32	37·8	56—17
A	33	36·6	48—24
F	25	36·3	47—19
J	36	36·3	55—23
E	40	35·8	50—20
C	30	35·7	49—20
D	40	35·6	53—18
K	38	30·6	50—17
G	15	28·6	46—17
	329	overall 35·6	56—17
		mean	

Music Achievement Test II

'The test was divided into two main parts: the first concerned with basic aural perception, the second consisting of questions based on a particular folk tune.

Part I

1. Melodies are played in which each beat (established by a metronome) is (or might be) subdivided throughout into a number of shorter beats (2, 3, 4 or 6). Children are asked to state how many notes there are to a beat.

2. Melodies are played which consist entirely of one of the following five rhythmic figures

Children are asked to decide which of the rhythmic figures is used in each case.

3. This is the same type of question as the preceding one but here the following compound time figures are used

4. Short passages of music are played in one of the following metres

$$\frac{2}{4} \quad \frac{3}{4} \quad \frac{6}{8} \quad \frac{9}{8} \quad \frac{5}{8}$$

Children have to decide in each case which metre is used.

5. The notation of 3 notes is given: F B♭ and E♭ labelled 1, 2, 3. Short 4 note passages are then played, using only those 3 notes, and children have to state which notes have been played, giving their answers in numbers, e.g. 2 3 1 3.

6. The notation of 5 notes is given—G A B C D, labelled 1, 2, 3, 4, 5 and 5 note passages are then played, which the children have to identify, again by numbers e.g. 2 3 4 5 1.

7. A diagram of one octave of a keyboard is given (C to C¹). Pairs of notes are played, one note followed by the second. The first is named by letter, and the children have to name the second.

Part II

The questions in the second part are all based on the Irish folk song *The Lark in the Clear Air,* the melody of which is given on the answer sheet in the key of A♭.

1) Choose which of the following words best describes the mood of the tune:
   Lively   Mysterious   Majestic   Peaceful   Energetic
2) Choose which of the following countries the song belongs to:
   Scotland   Russia   Spain   Ireland   France
3) State what time signature should be used (this is omitted from the answer sheet).
4) What is the key-note (doh) i.e. the letter name?
5) State the lowest and the highest note in the melody, giving both letter name and pitch name (sol fa).
6) Show the phrasing of the music by inserting V marks in appropriate places.
7) Refer to any places where a melodic phrase or part of a phrase recurs.
8) How often does the s—m—d pattern occur?
9) The tune is played but is broken off in the middle. Name the last note played, giving bar and beat reference.
10) Children are asked to write out the rhythm of the first half of the melody together with the given words, showing clearly how the words fit the music.'

It will be observed that in Test I only questions 9 to 12 involved visual association with the sounds heard: Q9 linear graphics, Q10 staff notation, duration symbols only, Qs 11 and 12 staff notation, both duration and pitch. In Test II, Part I involves some form of audio-visual association in Qs 2 to 7; Part II in Qs 3 to 10.

It is possible to evaluate very early stages in musical development without the audiovisual association, but, once those early stages have been left behind, assessment of achievement in music is almost impossible without this association: the ability to associate sounds with printed symbols, to 'read music'. Not only is assessment almost impossible, but so also is further development and achievement.

It should be remembered that these two achievement tests are not standardized, but only a part of a project that, at the time of this writing, is incomplete. One reason for describing them is to indicate ideas for assessment that others may improve upon. Another reason is to disclose some of the observations of the teachers involved in the experiment. Whilst by no means all were initially 'test-minded', after the experiment using Test I (Test II not yet having been generally used) there was general agreement on the following points:

The children obviously enjoyed doing the 'Quiz' and showed great interest and enthusiasm throughout. It was in no way a waste of their time; on the contrary they gained valuable musical experience from doing it.

'The enjoyment which the children clearly showed was comparable to that derived from games and sport. Just as a child naturally likes to measure his own weight, strength and athletic prowess in friendly rivalry with his fellows, so it is natural that he should feel the same about measuring his achievement in the field of musical skills.' (Thackray, 1974, p. 126)

The exercise was not only useful in measuring the children's relative achievement, but also gave to the teachers information about the strengths and weaknesses of their classes and helped them to see these in relation to their own teaching. Results indicated certain aspects of work which some of the the teachers had either not attempted or failed to cover adequately. Furthermore, the actual manner of presentation of the questions gave ideas to the teachers which they could apply in their own teaching.

The results gave the teachers increased knowledge about their children's musical development, and indications of realistic standards of achievement related to clearly defined objectives.

Such enhanced knowledge should result in more effective teaching and learning. Testing, formal or informal, can be a useful teaching aid.

Objectives

Evaluation is an indispensable part of effective teaching and learning. What is the use of teaching if we make no attempt to discover if the teaching is effective? The only way to do this is to establish objectives, and find means, which involves tests, of discovering if we are achieving the objectives. The first essential step is to establish objectives. Once we are clear about these, we can the more easily discover means for finding out if we are achieving them.

The earlier stages of education, up to, say, the age of 11 years, are not only the most important, but also more amenable to the establishment of specific aims than the later stages, when pupils' attitudes, and preferences, become more divergent and more obviously pronounced. I therefore append some thoughts upon music education in the primary school and some suggested aims, the achievement of which can be easily tested.

Aims and objectives of music education in the primary school— ages 5 to 11 years

1. The aim of music education is to introduce the child to music as a live experience, and, according to his abilities, to assist him to learn such skills as will enable him to take an increasingly active part in music making, and to become a more understanding listener.

2. Music education is *not* mere entertainment in which children have to make no effort. It is *not* the mere rote singing of unison songs, *nor* the playing about with pitch or other percussion instruments solely for the 'fun' of the moment—although immediate satisfaction at any stage is essential if further progress is to be made. *Neither* are the children there merely to be used as choral-singing or instrumental-playing material for teachers, or others, anxious to exercise their powers as conductors. School concerts and festivals have their place, but the learning of items for massed performance in public is only part of music education.

3. Enjoyment, both immediate and long-term, is important, but real enjoyment arises from the satisfaction of achievement at the level appropriate for each child. Linked with this, appreciation and aesthetic satisfaction come mainly through appropriate personal involvement in music making, which in turn depends upon developing skills and knowledge.

4. Music education can make a vital contribution not only to the life of the school community, but also to the personal development of the individual child. Well done, it can stimulate the bright child to even richer personal fulfilment and there is evidence that it can operate as a form of remedial treatment for the more generally backward. Elementary musical skills have only a low correlation with intelligence as measured by IQ; they depend largely upon rote memory. These skills can often be grasped and developed by the generally less able children, who thus gain in personal confidence, with the not infrequent result that their other work begins to improve.

In music, as in other spheres, children show a wide range of abilities at any given chronological age. Thus their individual rates of progress will vary, and not all will achieve as much as the most able. However, both general and specific objectives must be stated if the work is to proceed on a steady course. Some children may not achieve all these objectives; others will need even further stimuli and facilities in order to stretch themselves to the optimum.

The general aim has already been stated. It now remains to state specific objectives for music education in the primary school, i.e. what one could reasonably expect the majority of children to be able to do by the age of eleven years, given adequate teaching.

Specific objectives

1. Sing in tune with a pleasant tone.
2. Know by rote many songs:
    (a) Nursery rhymes, etc.
    (b) National and international folk songs.
    (c) Songs by 'classical' and modern composers.
3. Read vocally from staff notation (or other symbols) melodies, including chromatic changes.

4. Write in staff notation (or other symbols) tunes that are well-known to them, and short dictated melodies.

5. Play melodic instruments from staff notation, as appropriate to differing abilities and according to the facilities available; e.g. pitch percussion, recorder, strings, brass, woodwind.

6. Know some music through listening only, and something about orchestral instruments and about composers.

NB

1. Creative work (improvisation) would play an important part throughout.

2. Two or even three part singing is possible and desirable, but success in this depends upon some skill in reading (see objective no. 3 above).

Some primary and preparatory schools achieve these objectives, and in such schools music is a lively, exciting experience. The approach is serious and leaves no time for trifling, but that does not mean that it is either severe or humourless; on the contrary. However it does imply reasonably competent teachers, with adequate skills and knowledge for the stages at which they are teaching, with a clear idea of where they want to go (objectives), and with the means of testing to find out if their pupils have got there with them (evaluation). It also implies a structured, purposeful progression of work through the school; this need not be restrictive or rigid, but rather a core of work around which a teacher and pupils may be both imaginative and enterprising, but without neglecting the core.

Given such an approach, children sense a feeling of purpose and challenge, and, by getting stuck into the real stuff of music and working at it, they at least have a chance of forming attitudes towards music, and of gaining satisfaction and even enjoyment from it.

Because, as they grow older, the pupils' interests, preferences and attitudes become more pronounced and divergent, it is more difficult to indicate universal objectives for the secondary stage (11 to 18/19 years) of schooling. The main idea to keep in mind is that we are concerned with education and not mere entertainment, and that time is inevitably short.

If some of the objectives outlined for the primary school had been achieved, the secondary school staff would at least have a better chance of latching on to what had been done, and then continuing the process of music education during the first and possibly second years.

If 11 year-olds arrive at their new secondary school still musically illiterate, the only hope of establishing a sound base for further music education is to tackle this problem immediately the new pupils arrive, and press on with it during the first, foundation, year or two, before music becomes an elective (see pp. 25–26).

From the age of thirteen years upwards, I have suggested, music should no longer be a compulsory class subject, but an elective, either within or outside the normal time table of lessons. From now on the overall objective of the music educator(s) is to make music a live influence in the school community, for those who want it in any form, from the mainly academic through major performing groups such as choirs, orchestras, bands and chamber groups of any kind (string quartet to pop), to groups who mainly want to listen.

Given this kind of approach, young adults, like the primary school children mentioned earlier, also have a chance to form attitudes towards music, and possibly to derive satisfaction and enjoyment from it.

Chapter Five

Measuring Musical Abilities

Much has been written in previous chapters about the differing attitudes and abilities of children, of success, failure, testing and the position of the teacher as the servant of the child in school. All this stems from respect for the individual child as a developing personality. Respect does not imply a soft, sentimental approach to children such as allows them to do just what they like regardless of anyone else, their fellows or their teachers. They are not all angels. They need motivation, which may include prodding; they need curbing from time to time. But they are all individuals who are compelled by law to attend school. The implication of the law is that schooling will make a difference, which we hope means an improvement, both currently as individuals in the school community, and ultimately as individuals in a wider society.

The more the teacher knows about such individuals, the better is he able to help them both in the current situation and with an eye on their future. Ideally he should know enough of their strengths and weaknesses to challenge their strengths in order to increase these still further, and to assist them to overcome their weaknesses as far as possible; but he may have to admit that something, whatever it may be, sets a ceiling on what they can achieve in any particular activity; and let us admit that one such particular activity could be music. 'All children may be musical' but musical-ness is not distributed amongst all of them equally. Respect for the child involves acceptance that he may be relatively weak in some activities whilst, we hope, revealing strength in others.

One of the disadvantages of having to teach children in large groups or classes is that the teacher may not have the time for, or the means of, discovering enough about an individual child's relative strengths and weaknesses in order to help him to develop to the optimum.

An obvious way of discovering strengths and weaknesses is for the teacher to set aims or objectives, to teach (good teaching includes 'learning situations') with those objectives in mind, and then test in order to discover if, or in what degree, those objectives have been achieved. This has been discussed in the preceding chapter on Evaluation.

Tests of achievement provide information about what individual children can do under given teaching/learning situations, but that information is largely dependent upon the latter, i.e. the teaching/learning situation. How the child fares in these, successfully or less so, might depend upon something more fundamental, upon what we might call his 'potential', which may have some effect upon his performance in achievement tests. Whatever the cause, we have to accept that individuals differ in their responses to different situations, or to the same situation.

Is it possible to measure this 'potential for musical achievement'? If so, the information could be useful for the teacher.

During the present century a few attempts have been made to measure 'potential' for musical activities, or abilities from which potential might be estimated. In the USA Carl Seashore first published his 'Measures of Musical Talent' in 1919. In England Herbert Wing published his 'Standardised Tests of Musical Intelligence' in 1947. Again in the USA Edwin Gordon published his 'Musical Aptitude Profile' in 1965; and in England in 1966 my 'Measures of Musical Abilities' appeared. In the period between 1919 and 1966 a few other batteries of tests of musical talent, intelligence, aptitude or abilities were also published, notably in the USA, but the four mentioned are probably the best known and most widely used.

It is interesting to consider the titles given to these tests: They refer, respectively, to 'talent', 'intelligence', 'aptitude', and 'abilities'. The first three imply some kind of genetic predisposition that may condition future development or progress; the last, 'abilities', refers to what the subject (i.e. the child, pupil, student) is able to do at a given point of time. Such abilities *may* be interpreted as indicators of future development or progress, but they do not guarantee such. It is likely that they are a result of a combination of genetic predisposition, i.e. something innate, and experience or teaching. But, as has been pointed out earlier we cannot isolate these factors. The nature-nurture argument is so unlikely of solution that there is little point here in discussing it further. What we can do is to seek as much information about what a subject can do, and then, on the available evidence, and, as or if the occasion arises, interpret this, in as understanding a way as possible, in terms of 'potential'.

For the reader who wishes to know more about the Seashore, Wing and Gordon tests, the references have been given. He may also read in more detail about my 'Measures of Musical Abilities' (Bentley, 1966). However, because I can write with more intimate knowledge about the last mentioned, and because they have become so widely used, I propose to say how they came about, describe them briefly, give some of the results that have been obtained to date, discuss their use, abuse, and some criticisms.

How the 'Measures' came about

In the first place, I did not set out to make tests. Rather did I want to try to learn a little more about musical abilities, especially in young children before they had had much, if any, specific music teaching or musical training. Could I discover trends of musical abilities and how individual abilities diverged from these trends?

Obviously observation of individual children would form part of the operation, but in order to discover trends of abilities it would be necessary to observe large numbers of children under similar circumstances responding to the same stimuli; for this group tests were needed. In this idea there was nothing new. However, there existed at the time no group tests or measures that had been devised for children under the age of ten years. For most seven- and eight-year-olds in particular the existing tests were too long, or the instructions were not sufficiently clear; they had been constructed with older, more mature children in mind. Therefore it was necessary to decide what minimally (because of the time factor and period of sustained attention) might be measured and to present this in a manner that most seven-year-olds could understand. If such measures could be constructed, we might learn a little more about the abilities of young children.

There was much trial and experiment, and eventually four sub-tests were devised and tried out on groups of children from seven years of age upwards to fourteen years. It was discovered that most of the seven-year-olds tested could, in fact, understand the instructions; since they could understand, it was considered that most older children would also be able to understand. Obviously there is no point in continuing with any operation if the subjects are not clear as to what they are expected to do.

A brief description of the 'Measures'

A brief description of the 'Measures' is necessary for understanding the rest of this chapter, but fuller details may be read elsewhere. (Bentley, 1966). After observing what appeared to be the natural development of very young children in terms of musical sounds, their making of them, and their reaction to them; and after considering what are the basic elementals of music in terms of sounds and organization thereof, it was decided to try to measure (1) pitch discrimination, (2) memory: (a) tonal (b) rhythmic, and (3) chord analysis. The first three are essential to any grasp of, or skill in, music, whether Occidental or Oriental, in its most elemental form: melody. The last is regarded as highly desirable in view of the way music in the Western world has developed over at least the last thousand years. In the chord analysis test, the subjects are merely asked to say how many concurrent sounds they hear.

The 'Measures' were tried on many more children within the age range 7 to 14 years, and some norms established. The experiments had been done, and, in terms of what the tests measured, a little more had been learnt about the musical abilities of young children. Wider use of the measures through publication was not envisaged; but eventually they were published, and their much wider use in, and feed back from, not only the United Kingdom but also from some other countries has resulted in increased knowledge.

Some results obtained from use of the 'Measures'

These tests do not measure the *whole* of musical ability but four important aspects of it; this must be borne in mind as we come to examine some of the results obtained. It must also be remembered that we are dealing with human beings who, fortunately, defy too specific categorization or classification. Some figures are quoted and they are accurate for the subjects tested, but the number of subjects tested can be only a small proportion of the population as a whole, however representative we try to make it. Whatever statistical procedures we apply, we can never be *sure* that a particular sample of subjects is truly representative of the whole population. Thus such figures as I give are in the simplest possible form and based upon actual scores obtained.

It will be recalled that the object of making and using the tests was to learn something about the trends of the abilities measured and individual deviations from these.

From a sample of some 2000 children from 7 to 14 years of age tested in 1963–64, it was found that there was a gradual increase in mean (average) scores from year to year of about 5 per cent. The total increase in mean scores for eight years (from 7 to 14 years inclusive) was 40 per cent. In contrast with this, the average range of scores (highest to lowest) at each age was 66 per cent. Ten years later, during 1973–74, returns received from schools of different types in several parts of the United Kingdom show a comparable pattern: From a sample of 5,500 subjects (aged 7 to 14) the total increase in mean scores was 33 per cent and the average range of scores 79 per cent. The differences (40 per cent and 33 per cent; 66 per cent and 79 per cent) are of less importance than the trends they reveal.

The trends in both cases indicate a small average increase with age but at every age level a very wide range of abilities. Outstanding individual deviations from the trends are, for example, a six-year-old scoring 52 (out of a maximum of 60), a seven-year-old 53, a nine-year-old 56, a twelve-year-old 59. It is interesting to compare these with the mean score of 57 for 133 adult graduate musicians. At the other end of the range we find scores as low as 9 and 10 for twelve- and fourteen-year-olds.*

These trends, with similar distributions of scores, and thus comparable individual deviations from the mean, have been confirmed in data received from Japan: 3350 children between 7 and 14; Israel: 990 children between 8 and 14; in 1100 children aged 10 to 14 from West Germany, and 440 aged 8 to 15 years from Argentina.

Thus some 13,000 children between the ages of 7 and 14, from widely varying environments, show a gradual but small average increase in musical abilities (as measured by these tests) from year to year and very wide ranges of abilities at each chronological age.†

How valid and how reliable are the 'Measures'?

How much confidence can we have in these tests? How valid are they? How reliable?

How valid? Are they in fact measuring musical abilities? This is not an easy question to answer. In the first place validity is almost

---

* At each age the scores are normally distributed with standard deviations varying from 7·44 to 9·29.

† It will be realized that the figures quoted are the total scores for the four sub-tests of the battery; the sub-tests themselves show similar trends and deviations.

impossible to quantify with any degree of certainty. However it is possible to obtain some degree of assessment of validity by comparing children's test scores with the opinions of acknowledged expert musicians about those children's musical abilities, and by asking such experts themselves to work the tests. It is also possible to compare test scores with marks gained in achievement tests after a period of instruction and learning leading to specified objectives. If the opinions of expert musicians are in agreement with the test scores, or with the rank order denoted by these, then it may be suggested that the tests are measuring some aspect of musical ability. If the experts themselves achieve high scores, we may assume that the content of the tests holds their interest. If there is a high correlation between test scores and marks obtained in an achievement test that concentrates on musical listening and skills (as distinct from, for example, a test on dates of composers or other such essentially non-musical knowledge), we may again have some confidence in the validity.

All these, and other, comparisons have been made, all with a high level of agreement. The fact that the measures have become so widely used by musicians is another indication of confidence in their validity.

We now ask the question: How reliable are the measures? Do they, for example, produce comparable results when given a second time? If not, the results would be due mainly to chance; and whilst some element of chance is likely to be present in any test of human behaviour, we hope to reduce this to a minimum.

When 90 boys and girls aged 10 years were re-tested after four months, the correlation co-efficient was $r = 0.84$.

Another way of assessing reliability is to inspect the stability of the grades obtained on two occasions of testing.

Grading of scores

As a *general guide,* five grades were calculated (Bentley, 1966, p. 102) for each year age group, from 7 years to 14 years inclusive, as follows:

Grade A : top   10%
Grade B : next   20%
Grade C : middle 40%
Grade D : next   20%
Grade E : lowest 10%

It must be stressed that this is *only a general guide*. In dealing with human beings who, mercifully, refuse to remain absolutely constant in their behaviour, it is essential to interpret these grades intelligently, especially at the border lines. One raw mark in a child's score can change his grade; a difference of 9 raw score marks at 9 years could involve a change from grade C to grade A and vice versa. This is one of the hazards in any kind of classification; hence the great importance of not labelling a child permanently on the basis of one test.

However, it is useful to know how reliable the grades are, bearing in mind the remarks made above.

Five different groups of children, in different parts of the United Kingdom and coming from widely differing home backgrounds (including some immigrants), were tested twice at between 7 months and 12 months intervals. The total number of children involved was 315 between the ages of 7 years and 11 years on the occasion of the first testing. Some had had regular music lessons in the period between the testing; some had not. Regular lessons or not, considerable changes and development can occur in a child of any age during a 7 or 12 month period, and the younger the child the greater the changes are likely to be.

Detailed results of these testings and grade stability or movement are given in the table on page 96. Overall:

1. Forty-one per cent (of the 315 children) remained in the same grade through two testing sessions.

2. Forty-seven per cent moved only one grade (where a difference of a single raw score mark can change the grade).

3. Thus 88 per cent remained in the same grade or moved by only one grade.

4. Ten per cent moved two grades; and in the sample where the first testing took place at age 7 years, 2 per cent moved up 3 grades. The younger the children in any kind of formal test situation, the less reliable are they likely to be. For instance, the only movement of more than two grades was made by five seven-year-olds for whom a considerable amount of musical experience had been provided in the period between the two testings.

5. Where movement of grades occurred, the proportions were: upward movement 42 per cent; downward movement 17 per cent. This need not cause much surprise when we remember that on the second occasion of testing, every child was so much older, and, although he

Stability of grades on re-test

Source	No. of Subjects	Mean ages at testing		Stayed Same	Results								
					Moved One grade			Moved Two grades			Moved Three grades		
		1st	2nd	Same	Up	Down	Total	Up	Down	Total	Up	Down	Total
		yrs.	yrs.	%	%	%	%	%	%	%	%	%	%
1	99 g	11	12	50	24	13	37	9	4	13	—	—	—
2(A)	85 b&g	10	11	42	27	24	51	4	3	7	—	—	—
3(B)	31 b&g	9·9	10·4	42	33	15	48	8	2	10	—	—	—
4	50 b&g	8	9	46	42	10	52	2	—	2	—	—	—
5	50 b&g	7	8	26	36	10	46	16	2	18	10	—	10
Totals	315 b&g			206	162	72	234	39	11	50	10	—	10
Means				41·2	32·4	14·4	46·8	7·8	2·2	10	2	—	2
				41	32	15	47	8	2	10	2	—	2

(A) Bentley, 1966, p. 104.
(B) Including several immigrant children.

would be unlikely to remember the detail of each item of the test, he would more easily adapt himself to the test situation and more quickly grasp the instructions.

6. Most of the upward grade movements were from initially low grades, especially those moving up two grades. It is not so easy to achieve big upward movement from an initially high grade! But only 10 per cent moved two grades and only 2 per cent moved three.

Thus it appears from this evidence that there is only one chance out of eight that a child will move two grades on a second testing: e.g. from E to C, from D to B, from C to A, or, less likely, the reverse order downwards. One chance out of eight is really quite big. If any critical decision must be taken on the basis of test score and grade, and if these for example contradict the reasonable expectations of a teacher who knows the child well, then the test can be given again, or ignored! However, the general tendencies are clear: a child with an initial high score is likely to retain it, or move only marginally. A child with an initial score of E or D is very rarely likely to move to, for example, B or A.*

In human behaviour we can *never* predict with certainty about an individual, however well supported by statistics (which in any case deal with probability and not with incontrovertible *proof*); but the trends are clear.

Distribution of scores over a ten-year interval

The section on stability of grades dealt with the same children working the 'Measures' on two separate occasions. It is also interesting to observe how the scores of different children were distributed, one group in 1963 and the other group, ten years later, in 1973. During that period some changes in education, even in ideas on music education, may have taken place in primary schools. The graph for 1963 was based upon 360 eleven-year-old children in the Reading area; that for 1973 was based upon 961 eleven-year-olds in different schools in other parts of the United Kingdom. Yet the graphs of score distributions are remarkably similar, indicating yet again a comparably wide spread of abilities at the same chronological age. It would seem that, in terms of what the tests are measuring, the children in 1973 had similar abilities to those of 1963.

* The only instance of 3-grade moves upwards were the five 7-year-olds, 1·6 per cent of the total to date tested twice. At that age, misunderstanding of the instructions is more likely than with older children, and could account for the initial low grades.

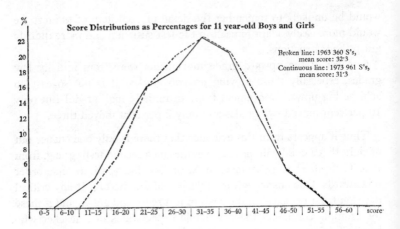

Some uses of the 'Measures'

(1) *As one means of selecting children for special musical experience*

Almost inevitably since the 'Measures' became publicly available they have been used by teachers as one of the means of selecting children for additional musical experiences and tuition, for example for instruction in the playing of string or wind instruments. Such specialist tuition is inevitably limited: There are not enough string or wind teachers to deal with all children either inside or outside school. Hence some selection is necessary.

Common observation reveals differing attitudes to, and abilities in, music; the 'Measures' give an indication of how widely those abilities differ. It may be maintained, *with due caution,* that children who score well in the 'Measures' are likely to make more progress, and thus achieve greater satisfaction, in special instrumental tuition and playing than children who score badly. Since personnel and facilities are limited it may be argued, not without reason, that optimum use should be made of such personnel and facilities. The teacher obviously prefers to work with children who are not only positively motivated but also who, as far as can be ascertained, are likely to make the better progress. (I refer here to the 'normal' school situation, not to the highly specialized fields of teaching 'slow learners' or to music therapy). Furthermore, children with little ability may quickly become discouraged in trying to play an instrument requiring greater than normal skills; and to put them into a situation where they are likely, on the available evidence, to meet with comparative or even total failure is to do them a disservice.

Admittedly there are exceptions: Private teachers are not un-acquainted with the unusual pupil who, in spite of minimal progress, insists on continuing with tuition. Reasons for such persistence are elusive. However the circumstances of the one-to-one teacher-pupil relationship in the studio or home are different from those of the school community, where the pupils are in close contact with their fellows and compare their own achievements with those of others. There is the additional difference in that the pupil, or his parents, have a direct personal contract with the tutor, which includes the direct handing over of money for services rendered. Similar 'services rendered' have to be paid for in school, either by extra 'fees' or through rates and taxes, but rarely does the pupil, or parent, make direct payment to the teacher; at this level there is less personal involvement.

Selection by mere chance, or passing whim, may include children with little ability, thus, because of limited facilities, excluding other children with much greater ability but who, possibly, were unaware of it. So it would appear that these 'Measures', or any other standardized tests of musical abilities appropriate to the age of the subjects, might have some use in the process of selection, provided that the results of the testings are interpreted with the due caution mentioned earlier; they do not measure the whole of musical ability nor do they measure other important considerations such as school and parental attitudes and encouragement, neuro-muscular co-ordination, perseverance. There is no *guarantee* that a child with a high score will even wish to take part in instrumental work. On the other hand a child with a lower test score, but keen, determined and with strong parental support, should not be excluded solely on the grounds of his test score if a place can be found for him. This is a matter of personal judgement for the teacher in conjunction with the parents and the child; and re-testing should not be overlooked.

Several instances of the use of the 'Measures' in selection for instrumental tuition, and other groupings, have been reported to me in correspondence with Music Advisers, lecturers and school teachers. All state that it is the children with the highest scores (in grades A and B, i.e. the top 30 per cent for their age) who continue to play and who make progress, and that, with few exceptions, children scoring in the C, D and E grades make relatively slow progress and before very long cease to play.

Mawbey (1973, pp. 33–43) reports on 448 boys and girls (330 in primary schools and 118 in secondary schools) who were given the

'Measures' when they had already started instrumental tuition, mostly on strings. He reports that 'one in every two children who began lessons on an orchestral instrument in 1969 had dropped out by the end of the fourth term of lessons'. (p. 33) The actual fall-out for primary and secondary children combined was 52 per cent. (p. 37) The fall-out for secondary pupils alone was 66 per cent, which corresponded almost identically with the 63 per cent who scored in the C, D, E grades of the 'Measures'.*

Ponsford (1972, pp. 10–12) reports briefly on the use of the 'Measures' with boys who had started tuition on brass instruments. Most of the boys scoring in Grades C and below 'ceased to learn their instruments . . . . Groups A and B show most progress'. (p. 11)

It would seem therefore that one of the uses of the 'Measures' would be to help in the indication of which children might gain the greater satisfaction of achievement in the more specialist musical activities such as instrumental playing.

(2)   *In assessing 'giftedness'*

Such children (e.g. top 30 per cent) might not unreasonably be regarded as at least comparatively 'gifted'. Yet it is interesting to note that in a book of 272 pages devoted to 'Gifted Children in the Primary Schools' (Ogilvie, 1973) in which 'giftedness' in music is discussed, the sole reference to any kind of *tests* of musical abilities is in the negative:

Violin . . . . children selected by ability (it is not stated how this ability is assessed) and enthusiasm of parents. Music tests as such are not used to identify potential musicians. (p. 254)

There is a whole selection of several pages devoted to the recognition of musical talent (pp. 73–82). There are three lists of 'features' of musical talent (p. 73), 'criteria of recognition' of same (p. 74) and 'distinguishing marks of the music prodigy' (p. 82). Coupled with this is the admission that 'a very large number of our teachers . . .

---

* Mawbey suggests that selection for instrumental tuition should start with a standardized test of musical ability for screening purposes, followed by an inquiry into the existing musical interests of the pupils who have scored highly, and of their parents, and meetings between the parents and Head of School or of Music Department and the peripatetic instrumental teacher, (p.42).

pointed out that they had neither the knowledge nor the experience in music to be able to recognize levels of ability, high or low'. (p. 74) There are seven case studies. Apparently in all of these the gifted child's introduction to musical skills was either 'fortuitous' (p. 75), or due to '*chance* exposure to musical opportunity' (p. 81) or to home influence (which might be non-existent or even antagonistic).

It is not particularly difficult to list criteria for 'giftedness'. Any group of musicians could do this and even agree on most of the detail. The difficulty arises in establishing a point at which it might be agreed that the child is gifted, and, above that point, how gifted: e.g. 'only just' or 'very'; and below that point a recognition that he is not gifted.

No one enjoys taking borderline decisions, particularly when the final decision must be below the borderline. But if the term 'gifted' is used, it must carry the implication of a minority having certain 'gifts' that are not possessed by the majority; and the implied dividing line between the minority and the majority must be clearly defined so that there can be no ambiguity in the minds of anyone involved in reaching a decision. Merely to regard 'giftedness' as a continuum between the highly gifted and those possessing scarcely any ability at all, which the book under discussion does *not*, but which some sentimentalists do, makes nonsense of the use of the word.

It is rather surprising that a book entirely devoted to 'giftedness' in children, including musical giftedness, ignores the well-known standardized measures of musical abilities (talents, aptitudes), the latest of which has been publicly available since 1966. It is true that none of these published tests claims to measure the whole of musical ability, talent, giftedness; but each one measures some aspects of it. And any one of them could provide a little more objective evidence to be added to subjective opinions of expert musicians, and even help the 'very large number of teachers' who honestly felt that they were not able 'to recognize levels of ability, high or low'.

(3) *For disclosing unsuspected abilities*

In fact one of the most valuable uses of standardized tests of musical abilities is that they sometimes reveal high abilities that would otherwise have gone undisclosed in children who had not previously had the 'chance exposure to musical opportunity'. Furthermore, sometimes such children come from unpromising socioeconomic-cultural environments. Without some such scanning test such children would be overlooked, to their disadvantage.

It is not easy to get busy teachers to report such cases; but a few instances have been reported back to me of cases where, as a result of disclosure of high abilities as measured by the tests, a child has been given opportunity for musical tuition and experience additional to what is possible in normal class work; and has (1) made good progress musically and (2) shown improvement in other spheres of school work and in general attitude as a result. He has found something he could do well, and this seems to have given him confidence in himself not only in music but outside it.

Summary

The objective of devising measures of musical abilities is to provide the teacher with a means of learning a little more about individual pupils in relation to their fellows. The greater the teacher's knowledge of the pupils' abilities, the better should be the teaching of the teacher and the learning of the pupils. The whole operation is undertaken in the interest of the pupils.

The 'Measures' discussed here at some length, and the others mentioned, provide information that could not be so quickly, perhaps even so efficiently, obtained in the normal course of class or group teaching, or indeed, especially in the case of the pitch discrimination test, in any other way. Because they have been standardized on large numbers of children they also provide the means of comparison with much bigger numbers than any single school could provide. In this respect standardized measures of musical abilities have a comparable function to standardized tests of achievement (see p. 77 above).

The trends disclose a slow and fairly steady increase in mean scores for the abilities measured from year to year, from 7 to 14 years of age. In contrast, individual deviations from the general trends are shown to be very wide at each chronological age level.

In terms of the grades achieved, the abilities of individuals appear to be fairly stable.

The distributions of abilities of children from different regions, and over a period of at least a decade, are very similar.

Children scoring in the two highest grades (A and B, i.e. the top 30 per cent for their age) seem to be likely to make more progress in instrumental playing than those scoring in the lower grades (C, D, E, i.e. the lower 70 per cent for their age), the latter tending to make little progress and to withdraw from the activity.

Thus the 'Measures' may be used, with the due caution mentioned earlier, as a part of the selection of children for musical activities requiring more than average abilities. They may also be used to disclose hitherto unsuspected high ability.

They should not be used for the purpose of pinning permanent labels on children 'musical' or otherwise. They are not revelations of destiny. When the results obtained from testing are used for decision making about a particular child's potential, those results should be interpreted intelligently, imaginatively and humanely. The measures are no more than a tool; tools should not be abused.

Some criticisms

My 'Measures', like the earlier ones of Seashore and Wing, have been criticized. Such criticism is a normal hazard of publishing any-thing; and whether one accepts the criticisms or not, they certainly make one think again.

Some years ago I wrote '. . . one cannot avoid the conclusion that the abilities disclosed are to a great extent innate'. (Bentley, 1966, p 101) Perhaps that was careless. Obviously the ability to understand the language of the instructions, the ability to write the single letter or figure answers required, the ability to count up to five (as in the tonal memory test), are learnt abilities. The baby is not born able to do these things. But the enormously wide ranges of scores for each sub-test suggest that something more than learning or experience may be involved. Perhaps I should have written, less baldly, something like:

. . . conclusion that some kind of genetic endowment may be a part cause of behavioural predisposition that is reflected in the test scores.

Further evidence to 'prove' that the abilities measured are not innate has been brought forward on the grounds that the scores correlate significantly with the socioeconomic level of the child, with IQ, and that they are by no means resistant to the effects of practice.

Correlations with socioeconomic level, and with IQ, are accepted. They are also significant, which means they could not have occurred by chance. But it is unsafe to imply cause and effect merely because two ranks of variables are statistically correlated. One would expect a tendency for highly intelligent children from good socioeconomic environments to achieve better than children who were not so clever and who came from poor or musically uncultured homes. But there are not a few exceptions, as indicated by considerable overlap in the scores: Some clever children from good backgrounds score badly and some not so clever from poor backgrounds score highly; these individual exceptions are extremely important. One of the main reasons for seeking trends is to observe individual deviations from them.

The fact that the abilities measured are not resistant to the effects of practice is not surprising. A good teacher would indeed be surprised if he set out to train children in a specific skill and obtained no improvement at all. That teacher would be equally surprised if all his pupils improved at the same rate and reached the same improved degree of skill at the same moment.

We cannot solve the nature/nurture enigma. Whether or not genetic endowment contributes to our individual differences, we cannot measure it in isolation. Neither can we reliably measure environmental influence in isolation if only for the reason that we cannot hold genetic endowment constant as between individuals.

The figures, and the statistical procedures, of the critical studies may be valid for the subjects studied. What is questionable is the interpretation of them. In social and human affairs and behaviour it is very difficult to *prove* incontrovertibly. The statistics may provide evidence that enable us to say 'It looks as though . . .' but rarely more than that.*

* For a discussion of the problems involved in research into motivation and achievement *vis-a-vis* social class, home influence and intelligence, the reader is referred to: Shipman, 1972, Chapter nine.

Chapter Six

Research in Music Education

In the foregoing chapters we have discussed attitudes, strengths and weaknesses, success and failure, education and entertainment, the value of music education, organization and administration, ways of participating in music (as listener only, as re-creative performer, as composer), the operation of music reading, some current 'forward-looking' ideas on music education, listening to contemporary music, fashions in education and the desirability of balance. We then considered evaluation and the measurement of musical abilities.

Some of the points of view expressed are the result of day to day observation, discussion with children, teachers and others; in other words, they are based upon general experience, and that is largely subjective.

Other 'points of view' are based upon research; this may be distinguished from general experience because it is conducted under more rigorous, carefully devised conditions and managed in as objective a way as possible.

In one short chapter it is patently impossible to describe at all adequately the research in music education that has been carried out even in England alone during the last decade, nor will this be attempted. However some thoughts on research may not be out of place, especially since there has been a considerable increase of interest in it in recent years.

Some indication of the amount and nature of the research carried out in the United Kingdom alone may be obtained from the list of researches presented for higher degree in universities of the United Kingdom given as an appendix to this chapter. From 1920 to 1974, there were some 75 studies successfully presented for higher degrees.* This

---

* There may be more than this, but it is not always possible to extract full information from universities or candidates.

number is tiny compared, for instance, with work done in the USA. Furthermore, much research is post-doctoral, and some is not even presented for the award of a degree; thus it does not appear in the list.

Whether or not all this activity, or even some of it, has beneficial influence on what goes on in schools it is difficult to say. However, the more we can learn about children's abilities, attitudes, their interaction with music, how they learn musical skills etc. the better ought to be our teaching and the children's learning.

A distinction should be made between research in music education and musicology. The latter may be concerned with people, but not essentially so. Its primary concern is knowledge of the subject: music; and this is usually research-based, sometimes highly erudite, often of assistance in the performance of music. It is a respectable scholarly activity.

Research in music education should also be scholarly, but, as distinct from musicology, its main focus of attention is people, young and older, and the contribution music can make to their education.

In the expression 'research in music education' the important word is 'education'; and education is primarily concerned with people: children (pupils, students—whatever we choose to call them) and their teachers. Note the order: 'children' first; then 'music'.

What is research? I posed this question to the members of the First International Seminar on Experimental Research in Music Education in 1968. The seminar members summarized their discussion on this question approximately as follows: By pursuing research we hope to solve problems, to find better ways of doing things, to find the truth, even if it disproves what we had formerly believed. We search out facts, arrange them as logically as possible, and then face them honestly. We must avoid the kind of educational research, so-called, that sets out to prove that 'my position has been right all along'. There are few of us who do not hold strong opinions, and it is by no means easy to accept calculated disproof of opinions that may be of long standing, or even dear to us. But this we must be prepared to accept if we are to be honest in research.

There are different types or methods of research. There is the philosophical method that might be described as the 'sit and think' type. It is to the philosophical method, or aspect, of research, that we must turn for our aims and objectives, as Colwell (1967, pp. 73–84) states: 'It is the responsibility of philosophy to point the direction for research; to identify specific problems; to agree upon meanings of terms and upon both areas and levels of achievement; to locate and give voice to the needs of the profession so that research is done which can be truly beneficial . . . . Problems may motivate one to search for ideas, but it is the ideas that should determine the research'.

Then there is the survey method, which often uses the questionnaire, or interview technique to discover attitudes, what people think or do, what provisions are made for music education, etc. The validity of the results of this method depends largely on the skill and insight of the interviewer or compiler of the questionnaire.

We also have the historical method. 'Perhaps one of the most unfortunate circumstances concerning man's interpersonal relationships arises from his seeming inability to learn from the past'. (Madsen, C. K. and C. H., 1970, p 14). How true this is in respect of, for instance, methods of music teaching. A little more knowledge of the work of former music educators might inculcate a modicum of modesty in the young, when they would discover that their bright 'new' ideas had been practised years or even centuries earlier. There is a firm place for historical research in music education.*

Now we turn to what may be called the scientific method which is used in experimental research. This is a currently popular approach, but a note of caution should be sounded. Allen Britton (1969, p. 109), in a paper for the First International Seminar on Experimental Research in Music Education. 'Research in the United States', pointed out a danger in it for music education in the USA, which is equally applicable elsewhere: '. . . young men and women seeking the doctorate in music education are tending to specialize in the behavioural sciences and to conduct researches of a scientific nature. The problem that presents itself immediately is this: Is the training implied in such programs best qualified to produce sensitive musicians capable of improving instruction in music in schools?' The answer must be no, if training for such research occupies a disproportionate amount of the time that could be devoted to the musical training of those who will become teachers.

Because research is regarded as academically respectable, experimental projects are increasingly included in requirements for higher degrees and diplomas; even sometimes for first degrees. Yet experimental research in music education is scarcely the province of undergraduates with no teaching experience; indeed, it is only a tiny minority of experienced teachers who have the inclination to acquire

---

* Two United Kingdom examples of historical research are Rainbow (1967) and Rush (1971).

the expertise necessary for experimental work, which is a highly specialized operation that is entirely different from, for example, the kind of operation involved in musical performance.

One justification for introducing into undergraduate or initial teacher training courses accounts of research relevant to music teaching, together with an indication of the techniques involved, is to open students' minds to matters that they had probably not previously thought about; to encourage them to think a little more deeply and critically than they might otherwise have done about their future work as music educators. However, one would not expect many, or indeed any, of them to embark on serious research themselves before they had had several years experience of teaching.

Research in education, and that includes music education, is a task for more experienced people, and for only a tiny minority of these. Most musicians and music teachers want to be involved in music and music making for most of their time, naturally and properly. Good experimental research usually seems to spring from a particular kind of inquiring mind that most musicians do not appear to possess; and why, indeed, should they? However, when an experienced music teacher does show evidence of such an inquiring mind, and wants to undertake research—not merely in order to obtain a higher degree—and is prepared to labour for hundreds of hours at tasks which to many musicians would be tedious (research being 99 per cent hard grind and 1 per cent inspiration), then one may expect useful and profitable results.

So far I have had in mind the individual researcher. Circumstances are frequently such that the researcher is working on his project on a part-time basis, whilst he earns his living teaching in school, college or university. He is thus working alone, or in the case of work for a higher degree, with his tutor. It is highly desirable that he should have contact with other researchers who have similar or comparable interests. These are unlikely to be numerous in any particular geographical area.

'The research physicist, the research psychologist, the research musicologist, are all accepted and valued realities of the academic world. The research music educator is almost non-existent, and where he does exist, he has to slip his research effort into an academic life compounded of everything from conducting a performing organization to supervising student teaching. Such an atmosphere is not conducive to significant research, to say the least.' (Leonhard, 1963, p. 31)

Leonhard's colourful statement still applies, although sometimes a student can now acquire a grant that will just keep him alive for one, two or even three years whilst he devotes his whole time and energy to research; he is relatively fortunate.

He is even more fortunate if he can work as a member of a team, however small, devoting its major energies to a research project. The advantages of team work are obvious: The individual can constantly sharpen his wits on other members of the team. A team of even two or three is likely to embrace a wider range of knowledge, skills and disciplines than any one individual.

Educational research is inter-disciplinary, drawing upon the knowledge and expertise of other academic disciplines, between which there often appear to be cracks, if not yawning chasms. Educational research must be prepared to leap over some of these cracks. William Sargant (1957, p. 10) speaks of 'walls': '. . . if progress and synthesis are ever to be achieved, in this age of increasingly departmentalized knowledge, someone has to risk leaping over walls into other peoples' (academic) territory'.

This means that the music education researcher must be familiar with at least the fundamentals of other relevant academic disciplines. Thus he has to know his way around in, for example, statistics, psychology, physics, and, increasingly—I hazard a guess for the future —neurology and biochemistry; possibly also history and its methods, and sociology. He cannot become expert in all fields, but he must at least know something about those parts of them that have relevance for his particular investigation. He must have had time to learn enough about these other academic territories to be accepted as at least respectable when he approaches them. There are obvious dangers in this operation of leaping over walls or cracks. In the past too many optimists have stumbled, or fallen into the cracks. The result has been that, sometimes, some educational research has been regarded with suspicion, if not derision, by individual experts in other academic disciplines. However the risk must be taken.

If the music teacher can learn something from researches in any disciplines or skills that will make his teaching more efficient, and thus benefit his pupils, the findings of research must be made available to him.

In order to be of value to anyone else, serious research projects must be reported in full, giving all the necessary detail, so that any other researcher could replicate the project. Inevitably such reporting, whether in thesis or learned paper, will contain some technicalities that may be incomprehensible to the busy teacher who is not conversant with them, although even in such reporting one could sometimes hope for more lucidity and less unnecessary jargon.

However, if the research has value in terms of practical application in teaching and learning, it must be given an opportunity to make impact as widely as possible. Such wide impact is only possible through a means of communication that is shorter and simpler than that employed in thesis or learned paper.

An article entitled 'The Teacher and Research' in *Educational Research News* (1970) describes the reactions of some teachers to research:

> Teachers said that they ought to read research findings, but this could only occupy a small part of their professional life. Some . . . said that research findings were often incomprehensible . . . too long, . . . biased in presentation or not relevant to their problems. Many teachers felt that they were often asked to take up new curricula and methods without being told what was the purpose of them.

These are reactions and ideas that we cannot afford to ignore. The busy teacher in school, dealing daily with groups of real-life problems of any age from 5 to 19 years, has little spare time and energy for reading long research reports that are sometimes couched in pseudo-academic gobbledegook, and heavily laden with statistical data that only the initiated can understand.

What the busy teacher needs, if research is to have impact on teaching and learning, is reasonably brief, lucid, straightforward reporting of the essentials of a particular piece of research, with reference to the much fuller reportage in the appropriate journals for those who want to pursue a particular matter further. On the basis of such 'digest' reporting the teacher could decide if the matter dealt with might have relevance to his own work.

The actual manner of reporting research is extremely important if it is to reach the teacher and thus influence his work in education. It is all too easy, and by no means uncommon, for the experimental researcher to use a form of literary jargon unnecessarily incomprehensible to the lay reader. It is equally common for him to become so taken up with statistical procedures that, from the point of view of a teacher facing thirty pupils, a down-to-earth, flesh and blood reality, the whole business seems unreal.

This is especially so when, after long and complicated statistical manipulations and arguments arising therefrom, the conclusions drawn are so obvious that the perceptive teacher could react: 'I could have told you that without going to all that trouble'.

Whilst busy teachers may be sceptical of research that apparently has little practical value for their work, they are usually quick to accept findings that may help them to teach, and their pupils to learn, more effectively. Research in education, including music education, should be useful, and be seen to be useful.

The law compels children to attend school; it is up to the educator to ensure that the children's time is used optimally (ref. Ch. I and IV). This involves hard thinking, and research can help in fact-finding that may assist such thinking and decision making.

One question that we might usefully ask is: In trying to provide music education for all children of school age, are we attempting too much with totally inadequate resources of both equipment and teaching staff? Are we thus in danger of neglecting the more talented musically, whilst providing something educationally insubstantial and inappropriate (if no worse) for the rest? Research might provide some answers on which decisions about future organization could be taken.

We need to learn more about maturation and development of young children, how they form concepts about music, how they develop musical skills, vocal and instrumental.

If in fact they (or many of them) are ready to tackle some musical skills at an earlier age than we had perhaps thought—as some research experiments suggest—then teachers ought to know this and act accordingly.

I stress attention on young children; it is in the early years of life that basic concepts and skills seem to be most easily learnt. Yet it is only in the latter part of the 20th century that the very young have become the main focus of attention of researchers. Historically, research in music education has been carried out largely by university and college teachers. The subjects of their experiments were, not unnaturally, those nearest to hand: university and college-age students. More recently attention was paid to school children, preponderantly of secondary school age. At last, in the last two decades, we have reached the most important subjects, the very young, and their development in relation to music.

Some indication of this direction of attention may be seen in the papers about their main research interests submitted by participants in the first three International Seminars on Research in Music Education. (1968, 1970, 1972) On the first and third of these occasions, each of which lasted seven days, there were only two main areas of discussion, each preceded by a major introductory paper. At the first seminar the two major topics were:

1. psychological learning theories and music education, and
2. predictive measurement of musical success.

At the third seminar, the two major topics for the week's discussion were:

1. research in music education with very young children, and
2. goals and achievement in music education—a problem of curriculum research. All these major papers and the ensuing discussions paid the greatest attention to the very young.

A fair proportion of the articles that have been published in the first four issues of *Psychology of Music* also indicate a concentration of interest in the musical development of the young child.

The increase in the number of studies about young children and music should eventually lead us to better understanding, and thus to better teaching and learning; but as yet research in music education is itself in its infancy, and we must not leap to too many conclusions. We know a little more about children and music, but there is much more that we do not know, and the more questions we answer the more we find that have not yet been answered. Such is the complexity of the human organism that our body of ignorance seems to grow faster than our body of knowledge.

However, even from our limited research to date, a certain amount of information has become available which I think we may regard as 'useful'. I give just a few examples.

In the field of measurement of musical abilities my 'Measures' and those of Seashore, Wing, Gordon and others, have revealed not only trends in relation to chronological age, but also a very wide range of abilities (in terms of what the various tests measure) at any given chronological age. This is useful information for the teacher. The implications for the teacher are that he should discover as much as possible about his pupils' abilities, using any means including such tests, and then appropriately challenge his pupils to develop their abilities to the optimum.

Another finding of interest is that from about 8 years of age onwards the abilities measured seem to remain fairly constant. This was seen in the stability of grades in my Measures (p. 95 above), and the idea is confirmed by Petzold (1969, p. 84). These abilities can be improved to some extent by specific training, but a child who scores very high at an early age rarely scores badly later, and a child who scores badly at 8 or 9 years rarely reaches the highest levels later. We do not know the reason, but if it is nurture rather than nature then we must look hard at what happens during the child's first years of life.

Children who do not sing recognizably in tune with their fellows, or who cannot 'carry a tune' vocally, are a recurring problem in the lower classes of school. They are often referred to as 'monotones', a not strictly accurate term but less denigratory than grunters, crows, growlers etc.

Using my 'Measures' (Bentley, 1966), I found that a characteristic of monotones, as a group, was that they scored significantly lower means in pitch discrimination and tonal memory than 'normal' singers of the same age, IQ and sex, but that they scored equally well in rhythmic memory. (Bentley, 1968, p. 53).

Joyner (1971) followed up this work and confirmed my findings. Then, instead of trying to improve pitch discrimination and tonal memory by listening practice alone, he tackled the problem from the angle of physical voice building, or vocal training, in which, of course, listening is also involved. He found that once he could achieve a break-through vocally, i.e. physically, not only did the child begin to use his voice with greater control and flexibility, but his memorization and recall of tunes (i.e. tonal memory which also involves pitch discrimination) also improved.

Joyner went a stage further: when teaching infants from 4 to 7 years of age, he started with many monotones. Finding that his young pupils had a much smaller comfortable pitch range than the ranges used in many songbooks, he restricted the pitch of their singing to that comfortable range, first getting them to sing with improved quality in that range, and then slowly extending it upwards. Gradually large numbers of untuneful voices came to sing in tune, with corresponding improvement in pitch discrimination and tonal memory.

Cleall (1970) investigated the 'Natural Pitch of the Human Voice' in subjects from 4 years of age to adults, and found that most hymn tunes and songs used in churches and schools are far too high in pitch for comfortable performance by the majority of singers.

These are not the only two, nor the first, to investigate these voice problems under controlled experimental conditions. We may say that we knew this all along; but how accurate was our 'knowledge'? And had we practised what we 'knew'?

What implications may we draw from Cleall and Joyner? Singing is an important part of music education, yet many class teachers, and student teachers, are unable, or claim to be unable, to sing. There may be other reasons for this, but could one possible reason be that we ask many of them to sing at a pitch that is uncomfortably high? This can be not only uncomfortable but actually painful, physically as well as aurally. What is painful for the adult may also be painful for children. Teachers, and students training to be teachers, should be aware of this.

Let me give one further example of a tiny piece of research that surprised some of the teachers involved in it. It is concerned with pitch discrimination and the terminology associated therewith, e.g. higher/lower or up/down or same. Children may be able to distinguish fine pitch differences at a very early age, but it is difficult to prove this until they can communicate with the person who is trying to find out what, or how finely, they can discriminate.

Each item of the test consisted of two sounds and the children were asked to state whether the second sound of each item was

> louder or softer
> higher or lower
> longer or shorter

than the first sound. These were tests of broad recognition and under-standing, and not tests of fine discrimination; for instance in the pitch discrimination test there was no 'interval' smaller than a semitone. The tests were given to 680 children in the age range 6 to 11 years. At all age levels the results showed much higher scores for loudness and duration than for pitch. There was also a steady improvement with age in all three tests, but the improvement in pitch was greater than in the other two. Many children at all ages were unable to say which of two notes was the higher. This may have been due to inability to hear pitch difference, or to failure to understand the terminology: higher/

lower. The former is less likely than the latter, especially as no difference was smaller than the semitone.*

It is obvious from these results that teachers need to teach the accepted terminology of up/down, higher/lower in conjunction with early pitch experiences. Experiments showed that children as young as four years of age can quickly learn these. Loud and soft, and long and short are terms commonly used in everyday life in the same sense as they are used in music, and there is no problem. But the musical use of the terms up and down, high and low, with reference to pitch is quite different from the everyday use of these words. Thus they must be taught directly, or some children will never know them.

Obviously these short examples are only a tiny proportion of the research that has been carried out recently, but they illustrate the kind of information provided by research that can be of use to the busy teacher.

In an earlier chapter (Chapter Three) I commented upon some modern ideas about music education and music, and suggested that before new ideas were widely adopted they should first be subjected to rigorous validation on small samples, if only to avoid possibly wasting our pupils' time and confusing their teachers. Research techniques could help in this. The validation might disclose where, if anywhere, such new approaches lead: What are the ascertainable or measurable results in terms of the child's developing interest, attitude, achievement and skills in music? Skill may not be a universally popular word among educators, but without well-founded skills no child will progress far in music.

Then we need carefully controlled research, in co-operation with classroom teachers, who may not be very expert musically, to discover how they might interpret some of these newer approaches, or indeed any approaches, and apply them profitably in the classroom with 30 or more children.

Another matter that music educators need to try to consider by whatever means, research or otherwise, is the definition of music (the subject or area of knowledge and experience in which they are trying to educate). Is music 'anyone and anything that sounds' (Schafer, p.53 above)? Where does noise end and music begin? What is—perhaps,

---

* Once children have the concept of pitch movement, and the appropriate terminology, many (most?) can discriminate quarter tones by the age of 7 years (Bentley, 1966, p. 109).

even more important, what is not—music? To that we might also add: what do we want to teach, and what of that is practicable in school?

Research can not produce clear-cut answers to all our problems, but because it is objective it can sometimes help us to clarify our thinking; and clear thinking is perhaps the greatest need of music education at the present time.

APPENDIX

Research in Music Education: A list of researches presented for higher degrees in the universities of the United Kingdom between 1920 and 1974.

1. MERRICK, F. G.   MEd   Manchester   1920
   'The place of music in school education'
2. LOWERY, H.   MEd   Leeds   1927
   'An experimental study of musical ability in school children'
3. NURULLAH, S.   MEd   Leeds   1927
   'A study of rhythm and psychological methods of developing regularity of time and stress in movement'
4. MACFARLANE, D.   EdB   Glasgow   1930
   'Tests in musical appreciation'
5. DRAKE, R. M.   PhD   London   1931
   'Tests of musical talent'
6. MAINWARING, J.   MA   Birmingham   1931
   'Psychological factors in musical education and in the musical development of the child'
7. JONES, G. H.   MA   Birmingham   1932
   'Music and education'
8. MEIKLEJOHN, J.   EdB   Glasgow   1932
   'Using Macfarlane's tests of musical appreciation, to compare the relative importance of different factors on musical ability'
9. VERNON, P. E.   PhD   Cambridge   1932
   'The psychology of music, with especial reference to its appreciation, perception and composition'
10. MCINNES, I. W.   EdB   Glasgow   1933
    'An investigation of rhythm'
11. PAYNE, E. M. (Miss)   MA   Bristol   1933
    'The problem of listening to music'
12. HIGGINSON, J. H.   MEd   Leeds   1935
    'An experimental investigation of the musical responses of school children'
13. DALE, R. R.   MEd   Leeds   1936
    'The use of visual and auditory aids in the class teaching of music'
14. FUSSELL, J. H.   MA   Bristol   1936
    'Music in primary and secondary schools, with special reference to its aesthetic and disciplinary values'
15. WING, H. D.   MA   London   1936
    'Tests of musical ability'
16. FIELDHOUSE, A. E.   PhD   London   1937
    'A study of backwardness in singing among school children'
17. MCLURE, A. G.   BEd   Edinburgh   1937
    'The effect of partial hearing loss on the school attainments of 200 children'

18. SIMS, G. F.   MA   Birmingham   1938
     'The aesthetic appreciation of music and its training'
19. ANDERSON, T.   PhD   Edinburgh   1939
     'Variations in the normal range of children's voices, variations
     in the range of tone audition, variations in pitch discrimination'
20. SILVER, B.   BEd   Edinburgh   1939
     'Music—Intelligence—English'
21. SYKES, J. M. (Miss)   MA   Bristol   1939
     'Ideals in school music'
22. IRVINE, A. J.   PhD   Glasgow   1940
     'The development of musical ability with special reference to
     aural technique and sight reading' (3 volumes)
23. LIVINGSTONE, Rose H.   EdB   Glasgow   1940
     'An investigation into the sex factor in musical appreciation'
24. MEIKLEJOHN, J.   PhD   Glasgow   1940
     'The application of musical tests to the study of individual
     reactions to music' (2 volumes and appendix)
25. HOOPER, C.   MusD   Manchester   1941
     'The place and scope of music in a modern state-aided
     educational system'
26. WILSON, E.   MEd   Leeds   1941
     'The rhythmic factor in musical education'
27. WING, H, D.   PhD   London   1941
     'Musical ability and appreciation—an investigation into its
     measurement, distribution, and development. A contribution
     to the psychology of music, using a new series of standardised
     tests'
28. HOOPER, C.   MA   Leeds   1942
     'Music in elementary education'
29. PRIESTLEY, E.   MEd   Leeds   1942
     'Percussion playing and recorder playing in school'
30. THOMAS, G. I.   MA   Wales   1943
     'A study of the development as a school subject of music from
     the beginning of the nineteenth century to the present time
     in England and Wales, with special references to official
     reports'
31. HILTON, E.   MEd   Durham   1944
     'The musical education of the community'   (King's College,
                                                  Newcastle)
32. BARNEY, ETHEL R. E.   MA   Reading   1946
     'An investigation into the development of musical ability in a
     selective central school, with special reference to the effects of
     age, intelligence and training, together with a plan for a one-
     year course of work in rudiments of music and musical
     appreciation'
33. LAWSON, DOROTHY A. F.   EdB   Glasgow   1947
     'An analysis of factors underlying the musical appreciation
     of untrained adults'
34. MACLEAN, R. C.   EdB   Aberdeen   1948
     'A short study of musical ability and its measurement'

35. CHADWICK, A.   MEd   Leeds   1949
'The perception of musical relationships by school children: an analysis of experimental data and a discussion of practical and theoretical issues'

36. PRIESTLEY, H. B.   MA   London   1949
'Aptitude tests for performance on the violinda: an investigation into tests of aptitude for violin playing'

37. THOMAS, G. I.   PhD   London   1949
'An enquiry into the development of a new method of class music teaching, based on the principles of Gestalt psychology'

38. NICHOLSON, D. H. (Mrs)   MEd   Durham   1950
'School music of today'   (King's College, Newcastle)

39. WYLIE, MARGARET F.   EdB   Glasgow   1950
'Does the systematic teaching of music increase the I.Q.?'

40. NICHOLSON, D. H.   MEd   Newcastle   1950
'School music today (with teacher training recommendations)'

41. BELHAM, N. D. N.   MA   London   1951
'An enquiry into the value of a newly designed electronic organ for class use in stimulating musical ability and appreciation'

42. JAMIESON, ROSAMUND P. G.   EdB   Glasgow   1951
     (Mrs Shuter)
'An investigation into the songs children know at the qualifying stage, and their musical preference'

43. COULTHARD, J. R.   EdB   Aberdeen   1952
'Oral ability in French and musical ability as measured by the Wing Test'

44. DOBBS, J. P. B.   MEd   Durham   1954
'The influence of music on retarded children'

45. CARROLL, B. J.   MA   Liverpool   1956
'Musical taste: an approach to the Measurement of psychological, cultural and musical factors involved therein'

46. DUGMORE, RACHEL Mrs (*nee* Lowe)   MA   London   1956
'Music in Education, with special reference to the London area University extra-mural tutorial classes'

47. RENOUF, D.   MA   London   1959
'The Teaching of Music in English Schools—Historical background and contemporary trends'

48. BRUCE, VIOLET   MEd   Leicester   1961
'Dance and dance drama in education'

49. BENTLEY, A.   PhD   Reading   1963
'A study of some aspects of musical ability amongst young children, including those unable to sing in tune'

50. RAINBOW, B.   MEd   Leicester   1964
'Musical Education in England, 1800–1860'

51. SHUTER, ROSAMUND P. G. (Mrs)   PhD   London   1964
     (*nee* Jamieson)
'Heredity and environment in musical ability'

52. SWANWICK, K.   MEd   Leicester   1965
'Popular music and its effects on the work of music teachers in schools'

53. CROSBY, G. B.   MA   Durham   1966
'History of the Song School'

54. CLEALL, C.   MA   Wales   1967
    'The natural pitch of the human voice   (Bangor and
    and its relation to musical perception'   Aberystwyth)
55. DAVIES, J. B.   PhD   Durham   1969
    'New tests of musical ability using quasi-musical material'
56. HICKMAN, A. T.   PhD   Manchester   1969
    'Musical Imaging and Concept Formation in School Children'
57. ROWNTREE, J. P.   MEd   Newcastle   1969
    'A critical evaluation of the Bentley Measures of Musical
    Abilities'
58. SERGEANT, D. C.   PhD   Reading   1969
    'Pitch Perception and Absolute Pitch—A Study of some
    aspects of Musical Development'
59. BOWCOTT, E.   MEd   Durham   1969
    'Music in Education: an examination of the proposals of Plato
    and Aristotle, together with a special consideration of their
    possible relevance to the present day'
60. TAYLOR, S.   PhD   Southampton   1969
    'The musical development of young children (with special
    reference to instrumental experience)'
61. THACKRAY, R. M.   PhD   Reading   1969
    'Rhythmic abilities and their measurement'
62. CLEAK, R.   MLitt   Bristol   1970
    'A Study of Educational and Social Factors in the development
    of Musical Ability in Children of different ages'
63. PAYNTER, JOHN   DPhil   York   1970
    'Creative Music in the Classroom'
64. SIDAWAY, P.   MEd   Cardiff   1970
    'Creative music-making by means of Orff Schulwerk'
65. SLOAN, WILLIAM B.   MSc   Bradford   1970
    'The Child's Conception of Musical Scales'
66. JOYNER, D.   MPhil   Reading   1971
    'Pitch discrimination and tonal memory and their association
    with singing and the larynx'
67. RUSH, J.   PhD   Reading   1971
    'The life and work of John Curwen 1816–1880—a study of his
    work in music education in Great Britain its historical
    antecedents, and its influence abroad'
68. KEMP, A. E.   MA   Sussex   1971
    'A pilot study of the Personality   (Educ)
    Pattern of Creative Music Students'
69. EVANS, JOAN M.   MA   Cardiff   1971
    'A Comparative Study of different approaches to the teaching
    of music in Junior Schools'
70. SWANWICK, KEITH   PhD   Leicester   1971
    'Music and the Education of the Emotions: A Study of
    Musical Cognition'
71. BAGGALEY, JONATHAN P.   PhD   Sheffield   1972
    'Colour and Musical Pitch'
72. ROBERTS, EMLYN   MA   Liverpool   1972
    'Poor Pitch Singing: A survey of   (Psychol)
    its incidence in school children,
    and its response to remedial training'

73. HALL, RALPH   MEd   Reading   1972
     'Effects of Training and Practice on three of the Bentley "Measures of Musical Ability" with nine year old children'
74. HYDE, DEREK E.   MPhil   Reading   1973
     'Part music for female voices, with particular reference to English Music of the 20th century'
75. SCHLOTEL, BRIAN K.   PhD   Reading   1974
     'A study of music written for use in education by some modern British composers in relation to the philosophy of music education'

BIBLIOGRAPHY

BENTLEY, A. (1966). *Measures of Musical Abilities* and *Musical Ability in Children and its Measurement.* London: Harrap.

BENTLEY, A. (1968). *Monotones—a comparison with 'normal' singers in terms of incidence and musical abilities.* London: Novello.

BILLROTH, T. (1896). *Wer ist musikalisch?* Berlin: 1896.

BRITTON, A. (1969). 'Research in the United States', *Journal of Research in Music Education* XVII (i) Spring 1969 pp. 108–111.

BROWNLOW, J. (1858). *History and Design of the Foundling Hospital.* London: Warr, pp. 91–92.

CHOIR SCHOOLS DIRECTORY Choir Schools Association. Ripon. First published 1925, regularly brought up to date.

CLEALL, C. (1970). 'Voice Production in Choral Technique'. London: Novello 1970.

COLWELL, R. (1967). 'Music Education and Experimental Research,' *Journal of Research in Music Education,* XV: Spring 1967, pp. 73–84.

COLWELL, R. (1970). *The Evaluation of Music Teaching and Learning.* Englewood Cliffs, N.J.: Prentice Hall.

COOPER, M. (1969). 'What makes a professional?' *Daily Telegraph,* 1st March 1969, p. 15.

COOPER, R. (1974). *Times Educational Supplement* Extra/Music, 1st February 1974, p. 70.

CURWEN, J. (1875). From a speech reported in: J. Spencer Curwen: *Memorials of John Curwen,* 1882, p. 155.

DAVIES, P. MAXWELL (1962). 'Music Composition by Children' 'Music in Education'. Proceedings of the fourteenth symposium of the Colston Research Society, University of Bristol 1962, ed. Grant, W. London: Butterworths, pp. 27–28.

DENNIS, B. (1970). *Experimental Music in Schools—Towards a new world of sound.* London: OUP.

DENNIS, B. (1972). 'Experimental Music in Schools', *International Music Educator* 1972/2, p. 20. (Journal of the International Society for Music Education. Office: 133 Carinaparken, DK-3460, Birkerød, Denmark.)

EDUCATIONAL RESEARCH NEWS (1970). 'The Teacher and Research'. Slough: National Foundation for Educational Research in England and Wales, May 1970.

GORDON, E. (1965). *Musical Aptitude Profile.* Boston: Houghton Mifflin Co.

HELMHOLTZ, H. L. F. (1885). *Sensations of Tone.* Trans. A. J. Ellis, 1885, Longmans Green. App. XVIII.

INTERNATIONAL SOCIETY FOR MUSIC EDUCATION—RESEARCH COMMISSION (1968, 1970, 1972). Reports on International Research Seminars:
1. 1968 at University of Reading, England
   in *Journal of Research in Music Education* XVII.i. 1969.
2. 1970 at Royal School of Music, Stockholm
   in *Bulletin of Council for Research in Music Education,* No. 22, Fall 1970.
3. 1972 at Gummersbach, W. Germany
   as Edition ISME Research Series No. 1, Bärenreiter 1973.

JAMES, LORD E. (1972). Bulmershe Lecture 1972. Berkshire College of Education, Woodley, Reading.

JOYNER, D. (1971). 'Pitch discrimination and tonal memory and their association with singing and the larynx'. MPhil thesis. University of Reading Library 1971.

LEONHARD, C. (1963). 'Newer Concepts in Learning Theory as they apply to Music Education', *Bulletin of Council for Research in Music Education*, No. 1, June 1963.

MACONIE, R. (1974). *Times Educational Supplement*, 26th July 1974, p. 12.

MADDOCK, I. (1972). *New Scientist*, 11th May 1972, Vol. 54, No. 795, p. 343.

MADSEN, C. K. and C. H. (1970). *Experimental Research in Music*. Englewood Cliffs, N. J.: Prentice Hall.

MAWBEY, W. E. (1973). 'Wastage from Instrumental Classes in Schools' 'Psychology of Music', *Journal of Society for Research in the Psychology of Music and Music Education*. Vol. I, No. 1, 1973, pp. 33–43. London: Froebel Institute College of Education.

OCCUPATIONAL HAZARD (1974). 'Music and Musicians'. Hansom Books, Artillery Mansions, 75 Victoria Street, London SW1. Issue 258, Vol. 22, No. 6, Feb. 1974, pp. 5–6.

OGILVIE, E. (1973). *Gifted Children in Primary Schools*. Schools Council Research Studies. London: Macmillan.

PAYNTER, J. and ASTON, P. G. (1970). *Sound and Silence*. London: OUP.

PETZOLD, R. G. (1969). 'Auditory Perception by Children', *Journal of Research in Music Education*, XVII (i), Spring 1969, pp. 82–87.

PLOWDEN REPORT (1967). 'Children and their Primary Schools'—A report of the Central Advisory Council for Education (England). London: HMSO.

PONSFORD, A. (1972). 'Measuring Musical Ability', *The Trumpeter*, Journal of National Schools Brass Band Association, No. 49, 1972, pp. 10–12.

PREVIN, A. (1974). *Radio Times*, 17th–23rd August 1974, p.9.

RAINBOW, B. (1967). *The Land without Music—Musical Education in England 1800–1860 and its Antecedents*. London: Novello.

READING UNIVERSITY/SCHOOLS COUNCIL PROJECT: MUSIC EDUCATION OF YOUNG CHILDREN. Unpublished survey.

RIBIÈRE-RAVERLAT, J. (1971). *Music Education in Hungary*. London: United Music Publishers.

RUSH, J. (1971). 'The life and work of John Curwen 1816–1880—a study of his work in music education in Great Britain, its historical antecedents and its influence abroad'. Unpublished PhD thesis 1971, The Library, University of Reading.

SANDOR, F. (ed.) (1966 and 1969). *Musical Education in Hungary*. London: Boosey and Hawkes.

SARGANT, W. (1957). *Battle for the Mind*. London: Heinemann.

SCHAFER, M. (1967). *Ear Cleaning*. Ontario, Canada: BMI.

SCHAFER, M. (1969). *The New Soundscape*. Ontario, Canada: BMI.

SCHAFER, M. (1973). 'Where does it all lead?', *Australian Journal of Music Education*, No. 12, April 1973, p. 3.

SCHLOTEL, B. (1973). 'Peter Maxwell Davies', *Music Teacher*. London: Evans Bros., Sept. 1973, p. 14.

SEASHORE, C. E. (1919). *Measures of Musical Talents*. (original 1919, but subsequently revised). New York: Psychological Corporation.

SELF, G. (1967). *New Sounds in Class—A practical approach to the understanding and performing of contemporary music in schools*. London: Universal Edition.

SERGEANT, D. (1969). 'Experimental Investigation of Absolute Pitch', *Journal of Research in Music Education*, XVII No. 1, Spring 1969. MENC Washington, pp. 135–143.

SHIPMAN, M. D. (1972). *Childhood. A Sociological Perspective*. Exploring Education. Slough: NFER Publishing Co. Ltd.

THACKRAY, R. M. (1974). In Reading University/Schools Council Project: 'Music Education of Young Children' also 'Some Research Projects'. School of Education—Music Section, The University, London Rd., Reading RG1 5AQ.

WELCH, L. M. (1933). *Making Music in Class*. London: J. Williams, p. 7.

WING, H. (1947). *Standardized Tests of Musical Intelligence* (original 1947 and subsequently revised). Slough: National Foundation for Educational Research.

JOURNALS

BULLETINS OF COUNCIL FOR RESEARCH IN MUSIC EDUCATION
University of Illinois
(especially Bulletin No. 22, Fall 1970: papers of Second International Seminar on Research in Music Education—Stockholm—1970.)

JOURNAL OF RESEARCH IN MUSIC EDUCATION
Music Educators National Conference, NEA Centre, 1201 Sixteenth St., NW Washington DC 20036.
(especially Vol. XVII Spring 1969 No. 1: papers of First International Seminar on Experimental Research in Music Education—University of Reading 1968.)

PSYCHOLOGY OF MUSIC
Journal of Society for Research in Psychology of Music and Music Education. Froebel Institute College of Education, London.